BETTER GYMNASTICS

HOW TO SPOT THE PERFORMER

BETTER GYMNASTICS

HOW TO SPOT THE PERFORMER

William T. Boone, Ph.D.

World Publications, Inc.
Mountain View, California

Library of Congress Cataloging in Publication Data

Boone, William T   1944 –
    Better gymnastics.

        1. Gymnastics—Safety measures.   2. Gymnastics—
Study and teaching.   I. Title.
GV461.B63   796.4'1   78-368
ISBN 0-89037-127-X

© 1979 by
William T. Boone

World Publications
Mountain View, CA

Acknowledgments

I would like to thank the following students, athletes, and instructors, who assisted in obtaining the photographs used throughout the text: Lisa Coram, Beth Holland, Deon Lee, Walt Thompson, Tom Forkner, Bill Dickson, Craig Jackson, Ed Morgan, Sandy Goodwin, David Bodenheiner, Cheryl Turner, and Judy Watkins. In addition, the author is extremely grateful to Deon Lee, Lynn Blount, and Walt Thompson for their critique of the manuscript.

Table of Contents

Introduction

Though many people know little about gymnastics, many admire the gymnast's ability to engage in highly intricate performances. This admiration is of such intensity that literally thousands of young girls and boys are intensely encouraged to become gymnasts as early as four years of age. I do not think that such an early age is absolutely necessary to produce an excellent performer within a reasonable period of time.

The real issue, which has a critical bearing on the future of gymnastics, is whether the individuals responsible for these young children are qualified and competent instructors. As with most sports, there are presently no regulatory controls over who can teach gymnastics. Anyone with any number of objectives can take charge of these children, using either a potentially dangerous approach to learning skills or a positive, realistic, and safe approach. There are many options and yet so little proper training and instruction in how to organize a class, a club, or a program. A teacher must be able to anticipate problems, utilize specific spotting techniques, and provide the student with a safe, progressive, systematic, and disciplined environment for learning gymnastics. As a result, the future of gymnastics is not really as solid as we in gymnastics would like to think.

We can help correct this problem by supporting only programs with competent instructors, as well as laying the groundwork for proper certification of gymnastics instructors and coaches. In this regard, the United States Gymnastics Safety Association has recently developed a safety certification program. This should help identify and correct the problem of poor and incompetent instructors. Although this idea may threaten some club owners and instructors, keep in mind that if we don't do something about it, our loss may be a child's life. It is that simple.

We, the gymnastics community, must work together to strengthen the sport and provide it the continued respect and growth that it and the participants deserve. This is a major reason for this book. It is written specifically to aid the instructor and coach of gymnastics. There is, however, a difference between this and other gymnastics books. This book defines the specifics underlying the *art of spotting* as opposed to a more traditional descriptive analysis of gym-

nastics skills. Many gymnastics instructors simply do not realize the inherent problem in teaching a physical education student, for example, the mechanics of a back walkover, if he does not understand the specific spotting technique physically necessary to help the performer through the skill. When physical educators and gymnastics instructors teach gymnastics without critically evaluating spotting techniques and safety considerations, they predispose students to a potentially dangerous situation.

Concerned leaders of gymnastics need to direct their strength, enthusiasm, and energy to the art of spotting. We must come to recognize that the "physical assistance" traditionally provided by a few coaches is not something they were born with. Spotting is a skill (actually a sport in itself) with certain prerequisites, such as muscle strength, endurance, neuromuscular coordination, mental programming, and the like, just like other physical skills. We must learn to use spotting techniques repeatedly to become efficient and safe gymnastics instructors.

It is hoped that this book will be of considerable help to beginner and intermediate instructor/coaches in both women's and men's gymnastics. In addition, undergraduate physical education students in either the gymnastics methods or elective courses should gain confidence in their ability to help each other in gymnastics classes, during individual workouts, as well as properly teaching students placed in their care.

This book offers a variety of suggestions for class and club procedures and organization; program planning; mental and emotional preparation; muscle strength, endurance, and flexibility training; biomechanics of spotting; and order of progression from the simple to the more difficult skills to aid the teacher of gymnastics. Remember, however, that this book is only a guide to help you. It is not and cannot be the answer to all the problems you may face in gymnastics. Whether you are a student or a teacher, you must apply these spotting techniques over many months to become efficient and confident in your ability to lead students safely through gymnastics. It is essential that you assume that the students are beginners and spot everything. The safety of the student is more important than the sport. In fact, the future of the sport is greatly dependent on the safety of the participants.

PART 1

THE BASICS

The Art of Spotting

Spotting is not a skill that is easily learned. It is as difficult to ascertain the specifics of spotting as it is for the beginning gymnastics student to learn the prerequisites of certain skills. Just as we in physical education have developed programs to teach and coach a variety of sports skills, we also need to address the fundamentals of specific spotting techniques. Physical education students, as well as anyone interested in the sport of gymnastics, should learn about the role of the spotter. We are thus coming to realize that spotting is a skill that must be learned, much like the skill itself.

Although learning how to spot can be compared to learning to shoot a basketball or to make a forehand drive in tennis, there is a major difference that must not be overlooked. If the spotter fails to aid the performer, that person may be subject to injury. It is obvious that this factor is not present when one attempts a jump shot in basketball.

After considerable practice, spotting, like any skill, becomes a learned process. Later, it may become an automatic response, depending on both the physical and mental practice of specific spotting techniques. Most interested instructors of gymnastics will reach this point. But this is not the end, however. Some spotters continue to develop what may be expressed as an "art." This final transition requires an unusually high degree of insight not only into the possible outcomes of a given performance, but also into the performer's anxiety prior to and during the performance. Moreover, there is an extra follow-through effect that one can visually understand and appreciate. This can be seen when observing the artist at work. There is always a motion of a hand, an arm, or the spotter's body, as a final thrust to the performer. The artistic spotter feels that the safety of the performer comes before his. This type of an individual aids in the maintenance of a safe and enjoyable atmosphere for learning gymnastics.

Principles of Spotting

Spotting can involve readiness to assist, offering a hand contact to give confidence, or aiding the performer through a skill. The beginning student, regardless of age, should be assisted through all skills to avoid injury and insure eventual success. As appropriate neuromuscular patterns are developed and the necessary prerequisites (such as muscle strength, endurance, and flexibility) are acquired, the spotter will assume a less dominant role in modifying the performance. Until then, however, it is necessary to adhere to the following principles of spotting to maintain the optimum interaction between the spotter and the performer.

Stand close to the performer. Get as close as possible to the performer. If, for example, a student is attempting a back handspring, the spotter should stand on the mat and as close as possible without disturbing the rhythm of the skill. The closer the spotter, the better the leverage; hence, the more effective the assistance. In addition, a close spot is easier and less fatiguing to the spotter's muscles and joints, especially those of the upper back and extremity.

Keep a low center of gravity. For the spotter to be effective in controlling and directing the performer, he must be stable when contacting the performer. The most obvious means of gaining control is to lower one's center of gravity. This is accomplished by flexing the hips and knees, and spreading the feet to increase the size of the base.

Be dynamic and alert. It is vital to the spotter/ performer relationship that the spotter be a dynamic person. The spotter must have confidence in him- or herself, as well as the performer. It is best if the spotter has a positive attitude and a sense of direction. To be less than dynamic and alert to potential problems is to ask for trouble.

- The concerned spotter should be a highly organized person.
- Skills to be learned should be discussed.
- Specific spotting techniques should be studied and practiced.
- The students' or athletes' abilities should be examined.
- Contingencies should be made for those students or athletes requiring special attention.

Such an individual is without question a tremendous aid to the teaching/learning process in gymnastics.

Communicate with the performer. The excellent spotter recognizes the need to communicate with the performer. Consider, for example, the comments a spotter might have to make to a performer attempting a handstand:

- avoid arching the back
- drop the head some
- raise the head some
- point the feet and toes
- straighten the arms and push out in the shoulders
- straighten the legs

The main point is that spotting is more than just a physical contact with the performer. The spotter is, in essence, the bridge between the known and the unknown. The spotter helps the performer realize, for instance, that her legs are bent while performing a back walkover. It is this type of communication that hastens the learning process.

Knowing when to speak out to modify a performance is sometimes a frustrating aspect of the spotter's role. The spotter's reluctance is usually centered around a lack of understanding of a particular skill. Therefore, to be an effective and safe spotter, the following points must be emphasized.

Skill progression. A logical progression of body movement from the beginning to the end of a particular skill is important for safety reasons. The spotter in the top figure, for example, failed to realize the importance of properly positioning the performer's hips over her shoulders during the upward motion of the right leg. This one oversight represents the basic difference between poor (and potentially unsafe) spotting and excellent spotting. Although the performer was assisted through the back walkover, she was not given the opportunity to develop the correct *kinesthetic feedback* to hasten the learning process.*

Skill analysis. In order to know when to intervene during a given skill, the spotter must understand the influence of specific body parts on the development of force that creates various types of motion. Again, referring to the previous figure showing good spotting technique, the spotter must acknowledge the importance of: (1) the arms and the head as they initiate the backward motion; (2) the support and extension of the

left leg to create the necessary reactive (or opposite) force; and (3) the upward motion of the right leg to transfer momentum. The spotter must also be able to quickly decide if, at any point in the sequence, one of these areas is dominating the others to a degree that will result in a poor execution.

Anticipation of injury. It is vitally important to anticipate when a performer is likely to miss during the execution of a skill. This is based on an understanding of both the performer's weaknesses and the more common pitfalls that break the rhythm of gymnastic skills. The performer in the figure that

shows poor spotting technique may have insufficient low-back and shoulder suppleness to arch backward to touch the mat. Other problems that may not be recognized as easily are:

1. flexing of the support leg, which distracts from the desired backward motion
2. a jumping motion just as the hands are about to contact the mat can place undue stress on the wrist joints, as well as preventing proper angular motion
3. prematurely lifting the right leg will result in a faulty foundation, since the shoulders will not be over the base
4. cervical flexion instead of cervical extension while arching backward distracts from the desired curve of the lumbar spine

These are just some of the possibilities that a spotter must be able to anticipate when spotting this particular skill.

The Dilemma of the Spotter

Most spotters realize that they have a tremendous responsibility in aiding the performer through a skill safely. The concerned spotter is fully involved, mentally and physically, in the spotting process—the step-by-step hand and foot combinations required for given skills. The manner in which these combinations are effectively employed may be referred to as the *runoff aspects* of spotting. The spotter should always be

---

Kinesthetic feedback is the perception or feeling associated with the position of one's body parts in space. It involves internal and external tensions, as well as forces that control the joints.

analyzing his influence on the performer. If too much pressure, for example, is exerted in positioning the performer, then the performer may not gain the insight for a productive workout. On the other hand, the spotter should not disregard extraneous body movements in an effort to give the performer the full opportunity to perform. The spotter must determine at what points in the sequence it becomes necessary to aid specific parts of the body, or motions absent or poorly directed. The role of the spotter is indeed a challenging one.

In practice or teaching class periods, the uncoordinated activity of the performer can result in slight or serious harm to the spotter. This aspect of spotting must be accepted, or one should not assist in the learning process. It takes an exceptional person to receive several blows to the head or face and still continue aiding the performer by such a comment as, "Hey, don't worry about it. You did much better that time." Although this is a productive attitude, it can be abused. When it is abused, the problem is most often a lack of proper thinking on the part of the performer, and not necessarily lack of physical skill.

It is important for physical education students and athletes to know that gymnastics is more than a physical training session. Although the spotter is responsible for the safety of the skill, the performer must be held responsible for his actions. If a performer avoids thinking about the correct motion of an arm or leg when this lack of control can result in harm to the spotter, then the performer must not continue. Otherwise, in time, the spotter will get hurt, possibly very seriously.

This causes a dilemma, since the spotter feels responsibility for the performer, while at the same time tries to avoid being injured. The performer should realize the sacrifice the gymnastics leader is making over other sports teachers who do not have to deal with this difficulty.

Teacher abuse can be as simple as a performer expecting the spotter to spot him over and over as though that is his job. Though such an attitude is prevalent among many athletes, students are generally less physically demanding. But while students may not expect the instructor to spot every move, their poor executions often result in considerable harm to the face and back of the spotter. The author has received blows (from the performer's elbow when spotting a front handspring) to the face and ears that have required four to six week to heal. The main point of this discussion, however, is that the performer can prevent unnecessary injury to the spotter by thinking through the performance.

Spotting elbow. A dedicated teacher/spotter is always subject to chronic strain, particularly in the elbow and shoulder joints. The weight of the performer's body must be counteracted via muscles of the upper extremity. Since accumulative tension about the elbows can become very great, tears at the points of origin of the forearm flexors can create tenderness, pain, and sometimes a loss of motion. We will refer to this condition as "spotting elbow."*

Pain on the *medial* (inside) part of the elbow appears to result from the stress placed at the *distal* (hand) end of the arm. The force is transmitted via the forearm *flexor-pronator muscles* to their respective points of origin. These muscles are primarily responsible for flexing the wrist joints. They are important stabilizers of the wrist (or hand), especially when the hand must be maintained in a certain position (as when supporting a performer). The forearm flexors also help the arm flexors during moments of elbow flexion or stabilization. Thus, these muscles are very heavily used when spotting.

Although this type of *epicondylitis* can become a serious problem with calcification or spur formation over the *epicondyle*, the pain usually subsides when

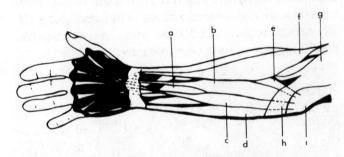

Flexor-pronator muscles of the right forearm. Most of these muscles originate from the medial epicondyle of the humerus. (a) flexor digitorum superficialis; (b) flexor carpi radialis; (c) palmaris longus; (d) flexor carpi ulnaris; (e) pronator teres; (f) brachioradialis; (g) biceps brachii; (h) bicipital aponeurosis; (i) medial epicondyle.

the frequency of spotting contacts is reduced.** If, however, the spotter continues spotting large numbers of students, the pain will usually become evident in both elbows. Eventually, the elbows will hurt enough to reduce enjoyment of assisting others. More importantly however, as the pain becomes worse, the safety of the participants is threatened. When this happens, it is important to know when to stop spotting, reduce

*See also Boone, Tommy, "Helping Hand Can Equal Sore Elbow," *The Physician and Sportsmedicine* 4(1976):42-44.

**Epicondylitis* is inflammation of the muscular tissues arising from the epicondyle of the humerus. *Medial epicondylitis* involves an inflammation of the points of origin of the flexor-pronator muscles of the forearm, due to acute or chronic strain.

the number of assists, or have an assistant share the burden.

Treatment depends on the degree of pain felt by the spotter. If possible, the problem should be prevented to avoid unnecessary complications at a later time. Some recommendations for preventing the condition from becoming chronic, and for treating the pain, follow.

The performer. A teacher or coach should not continually assist a performer through a front walkover, for example, if she does not work on flexibility exercises. Otherwise, the performer is asking the spotter to carry her through the move instead of merely assisting her. The teacher should discourage the attitude that the teacher's role is always to aid students. The performer must accept the responsibility of acquiring the necessary prerequisites for a given skill. Among others, these prerequisites include: muscle strength, muscle endurance, flexibility, a positive attitude, and confidence.

Spotting technique. By using two spotters simultaneously, the work load on any one person can be reduced, while still adequately assisting the performer. It is imperative that the spotters cooperate to avoid antagonistic activity. The more often the two spotters work together, the more automatically and functionally the technique will become. The muscles used to facilitate the movement become more controlled as the people involved perfect the interplay between forces aiding and inhibiting movement.

Another very important spotting technique is to *pronate* the hand (place the palm downward) and use the forearm extensor muscles. These muscles arise from the lateral epicondyle (outside) of the elbow joint. With practice, the spotter becomes as efficient as he was with the palm of the hand facing upward. With the force on the extensor side of the forearm, the tendons of the forearm flexors can rest to some extent, and perhaps begin the slow healing process.

When the spotter uses the arms and hands outstretched, as in the above figure, the forces pressing down on the arms must be counteracted by proper stabilization of the spotter. The muscles controlling the position of the *scapulae* are extremely important for effective control of the arms. Moreover, as the spotter flexes at the hips when reaching for a performer, the lower back muscles contract to maintain an upright position. The interplay among the spotter's arms, shoulders, back, thighs, and legs is very important. During an assist, the spotter's movements must allow for a productive assist, while preserving the symmetrical relationship of the actively involved muscle.

Rest. By removing the stress factor, one would naturally expect the elbow pain to disappear. But unfortunately, many teachers and coaches are unable to step back and let others do their work. Such individuals usually continue the struggle until the damage is too great to be corrected simply by rest. Most instructors realize they must reduce stress to avoid medical intervention. Sometimes it is necessary to apply local heat by *diathermy* or an electric pad.* When possible, a whirlpool may prove useful.

Medical intervention. With chronic or severely recurrent pain, local injections of the proper anesthetic plus a corticoid preparation are often helpful. If acute pain persists, it may be advisable to surgically disconnect muscle with obvious tears that is not healing correctly. The scar formation subsequent to surgery may aid in relieving chronic pain.

Don H. O'Donoghue, a professor of orthopedic surgery, writes in his book *Treatment of Injuries to Athletes* that local corticoid preparations should be injected into the area of tenderness to relieve the symptoms. In the case of epicondylitis, this area is the elbow. He further suggests that should the pain persist, then ". . .a second or even a third or fourth injection may be necessary to obtain permanent relief." He points out that it is important not to inject the steroid into the tendons associated with joints to avoid death of tendon tissue.* *

Repeated local injections of antiinflammatory steroids are used to reduce pain and allow for an earlier return to sports training or competition. The major point to understand is that the pain is a result of damage to specific tendinous tissues about a joint, and that these tissues should be allowed adequate time for proper recovery and healing. Use of cortisone for relief of pain may be desirable, especially when the pain is severe and disabling. However, repeated local injections to avoid missing competition is questionable and potentially dangerous.

Repeated use of corticosteroids may also bring about degenerative changes in the tendons, thus inducing more frequent ruptures. This was examined by researching the effect of varying dosages of a locally injected antiinflammatory steroid on selected biomechanical properties of rat tail tendons.* * *

---

*Diathermy is the generation of heat in body tissue by electric currents for medical purposes.

** Don H. O'Donoghue, *Treatment of Injuries to Athletes* (Philadelphia: W.B. Saunders Company, 1970) Second Ed., p. 233.

*** Murray B. Plotkin et al., "Dose-response effects of anti-inflammatory steroid injections on mechanical properties of rat tail tendons," *Medicine and Science in Sports*, 8(1976):230-34.

Although the research failed to demonstrate a statistically significant correlation between the injection and predisposition to subsequent rupture, coaches should nonetheless use caution when considering cortisone injections for a performer.

The concerned coach should realize that the injury may be the result of several factors: poor technique, poor training practices, or simply an injury that "happened." The point is that the coach should consider the performer's health, and not merely intense need to struggle in the face of an injury. Neither the sport nor the coach can be allowed to abuse the performers.

2

Conditioning

Gymnastics requires a considerable degree of physical fitness. As a result, the gymnast, man or woman, is more flexible and stronger than the average person. The increased fitness level aids in the execution of the gymnastic skills. And when the strength of specific muscles begins to lessen, the chances of injury are increased. Thus, it makes good sense to increase one's muscle strength and flexibility to cope with the mechanics of sports skills, as well as to help avoid injury.

The spotter must be strong as well. In women's gymnastics, women are just as effective spotters as men are in men's gymnastics. Concern for muscle strength, however, is essential for the gymnastics student. It is important that the performer train properly to avoid situations where the spotter has to sacrifice himself due to a student's poor state of fitness. This is an important, yet seldom discussed, point in most undergraduate gymnastic classes. But students must be interested in overcoming their deficiencies in fitness to improve their gymnastic skills. Hence, gymnastics students must work on specific skills that increase muscular power and joint flexibility.

The material in this chapter will help the student and gymnast to build or maintain the desired fitness level necessary to prevent injuries and attain top performance. In case a given performer wants to concentrate separately on strength or flexibility exercises, the two areas are presented in separate sections. There is also additional material on muscular endurance, coordination, weight control, and psychological preparation that the gymnastics student may find interesting and beneficial.

The principle of specificity applies to every conditioning program. The student or gymnast must address the particular weakness that keeps a given skill from developing correctly, and then design a conditioning program that will bring the deficiency up to par.

Endurance

Endurance can be subdivided into local muscle endurance and cardiorespiratory endurance. The first is concerned with the endurance potential of specific muscle groups, while the latter refers to the ability of the heart and lung system to perform for prolonged periods and to recover quickly on cessation of the activity. The competing gymnast may be well advised to adhere to training guidelines for both local and general endurance. But the gymnastics student should be particularly concerned with local muscle endurance, that is, the ability to use specific muscle groups repeatedly in a single teaching session. Increased capacity to use the muscles specific to a given skill or sequence increases the chances of learning it.

Local muscle endurance can be increased by progressively repeating skills or sequences, regardless of how basic they appear. As the sequence becomes more complex and energy absorbing, there should be appropriate rest intervals to prevent premature fatigue of the exercised muscles. The training program must be progressive and systematic to ensure that the muscles are challenged to their fullest.

Strength

The ability to do work against resistance is sometimes referred to as strength. This resistance to motion depends on the weight of the body, as well as the internal resistance created by the lack of (1) flexibility, and (2) proper neuromuscular interplay between the *agonist* and the *antagonist* muscle groups.*

Although various skills may be performed by the weakest of young girls and boys, it is logical that strength becomes more important as the difficulty of the skills increases. As a result, to learn intermediate and advanced skills, the concerned participant must rely heavily on strength training.

Some of the more common exercises for developing the upper extremity, chest, and trunk flexors are presented here. When necessary, depending on the particular concerns of the participant, the coach or teacher should consider a more in-depth analysis of strength training procedures in books written specifically on this subject.

---

*The *agonist*, or *mover*, is the muscle responsible for movement. The *antagonist* is the muscle whose action provides opposition for a particular agonist.

ability to consciously relax and avoid involving those muscles unneeded for a given performance. This aspect of conditioning is no doubt the secret of success for many world-class competitors.

Weight Control

There is no question that a gymnast or student should not be overweight when engaging in gymnastics. The excess weight results in a waste of energy, as well as an unnecessary stress on the performer's joints and ligaments. Imagine the difficulty of teaching the fundamentals of a handstand, and adding the extra factor of excess weight. The performer must be able to support the body and do so fairly comfortably. Excess weight distracts from the mental training needed for learning sports skills. It becomes increasingly difficult to concentrate on pointed toes and feet, straight legs, a tight abdomen, pushed out shoulders, straight arms, or any other things when excess weight must be counteracted.

Hence, I feel that an eight-year-old who is overweight should not be allowed to participate in gymnastics. However, every teacher or coach must decide for himself the approach to take. It is important to remember that acceptance of an overweight student or athlete in a gymnastics program should involve a specialized learning approach. The skills must be presented slowly, with plenty of support from the spotters, to avoid stressing joints beyond their safe limit. This approach may allow for earlier participation of slightly overweight children without exposing them to unreasonable physical stress.

To lose weight, it is necessary to:

- reduce the number of kilocalories consumed per day by not eating as much food
- keep food consumption fairly constant, and increase the expenditure of energy via involvement of large muscle groups in such activities as running, cycling, swimming, and walking for a reasonably long period of time (for example, twenty-five to thirty-five minutes a day)

Psychological Preparation

A student or athlete who devotes considerable study to conditioning, but neglects attaining a positive attitude, will have difficulty succeeding in sports. It is important for the performer to realize that both champion athletes and performing students must "think" and "feel" like a champion in order to win and perform safely.

Negative mental thoughts are useless, and often predispose the performer to unsafe performances. It is

also very stressful for a spotter to hear students say, "I can't do this." Too often students allow negative feelings to undermine their true potential. Hence, it is important that students and athletes understand the relationship between attitude and performance.

The teacher should encourage beginning students to engage only in those skills that can be safely performed. As the basics are learned, students will automatically feel more confident. The opposite is likely to occur when either the student or the teacher is too eager to attempt more difficult skills and combinations. Hence, the first step in psychological preparation involves learning skills within the performer's ability.

Should a physical weakness become evident, both the teacher and student must do something constructive about it. For example, if the arms are too weak to support the body when attempting a handstand, a strength program should be initiated to increase strength in arms and shoulders. By correcting the obvious physical problems, the performer will be better prepared. If the performer avoids correcting the problem, anxiety will be associated with execution of the skill. With the increased anxiety and the physical weakness of the body, the skill becomes nearly impossible. These factors not only prolong the learning process, but may predispose the performer to an injury.

The teacher should help students adjust emotionally to the new surroundings, as well. He can do this by actively involving himself verbally with the students. Favorable comments, such as "That was really good" or "You're getting much stronger," will help keep the performer motivated and interested in training. Such comments will help to shape the student's thinking, especially toward a more positive and realistic attitude.

The coach must approach gymnasts in much the same way as the gymnastics teacher. He should not assume that athletes are emotionally mature or prepared for intense training and competition. In fact, the coach should inform the gymnasts just what is expected of them during training and competition. If they know, for example, that a missed routine does not mean that they are useless or that they let the team down, then that portion of their psychological energy may be better spent on the actual performance.

Beginning competitors should expect to be nervous when performing before spectators, but these feelings will gradually lessen or disappear altogether. They should know where to sit, how to stand when approaching the competitition area, and how to leave the area when the performance is finished. These are all small but insignificant points of concern, as they affect the emotions of the performer. The coach is responsible for guiding the competitor through these areas.

The coach can, in essence, quietly guide the psychological preparation of the athlete. Such a task, however, requires a mature and understanding person—one who can work both physically and emotionally with young people. Lastly, the coach must be able to anticipate problems, and perhaps plan a less threatening approach to learning a skill to avoid excessive anxiety and frustration. The performer, in turn, must be open and willing to work with the coach. He must allow adequate time to develop physically, and must be emotionally open to guidance. These factors will enhance preparedness beyond a mere physical understanding of a skill.

1 Dips

This exercise is useful in developing: the triceps brachii muscle (1) that extends the elbow joint; the anterior deltoid muscle (2) that aids in flexion of the shoulder joint; and the pectoralis major muscle (3) that aids in flexion, extension, inward rotation, and *adduction* of the arm.* (The above numbers correspond to those in the figures. The same is true for photographs appearing later in the book.) By practicing this exercise, these muscles get stronger, thus allowing for more motions specific to the shoulder joint. In addition, it is easier to keep the elbow joint straight or extended when the posterior aspect of the arm is very strong. Without strong arm and shoulder muscles, skills such as the bent-arm press to the handstand on the parallel bars and the rings, and maintenance of a correct straight-arm swing on the parallel bars would be very difficult.

Adduction refers to moving an arm or a leg toward the body.

2 Chins

This exercise also develops the muscles of the upper extremities. To flex the elbow joints, the biceps brachii (1) must contract. This muscle, plus a muscle that cannot be seen, the brachialis, are the two primary elbow flexors. Thus, to pull oneself up into the rings, as during a muscle-up, these muscles have to be strong enough to counteract the effect of gravity. To aid during the upward motion, however, other muscles come into play as well.

For example, the pectoralis major muscle (2) and the latissimus dorsi muscle (3) contract to move the arm through shoulder extension while the body is moved upward.

3 Curls

The performer is often told to work out with weights to place a load on the muscles that results in muscle enlargement and an increase in strength. In this case, one can see the pronounced use of the biceps brachii (3) in creating the desired elbow flexion. The forearm flexors (5) also help in flexing the elbows. However, their major function is to create the tension necessary to maintain a safe and controlled grip on the bar. This exercise is good for maintaining and building elbow and wrist strength. This exercise also helps in developing the anterior chest wall, pectoralis major (1), stabilizing the shoulder joint through development of the deltoid muscle (2), and pelvic stabilization via enhancement of the rectus abdominis (4).

4 Triceps Extensor

Through the use of dumbbells, one can condition an isolated muscle group. For example, the dumbbell in figure 2.4 is supported through muscular contraction of both the forearm flexors and extensors. Some of the extensors of the upper extremity are above the elbow joint—the triceps brachii (2)—and some below the elbow joint—the forearm extensors (1). The triceps brachii aids in control of grip on the weight, and the forearm extensors allow for straightening of the elbow joint. The deltoid muscle (3) contracts during this exercise to aid in stabilization of the shoulder joint. Since both the teres major (4) and the latissimus dorsi (5) insert on the inside of the humerus (the bone of the arm), they are stretched in the position in the figure. This is a good position to strengthen these muscles, particularly if the arm is even more vertical or "hyperflexed."

5 Pectoral and Arm Developer

This exercise will develop the anterior chest wall, shoulders, and elbow extensors. Note that when the arm is extended, the triceps brachii (1) must contract (i.e., the muscle on the posterior aspect of the arm). Also, since the arm moves through what is called horizontal flexion, the clavicular fibers of the pectoralis major (2) contract. Thus, this exercise is beneficial for

upper body development. Take, for example, an exercise such as the front drop into an immediate straddle-cut to a rear support. This type of transition requires a powerful push from the floor to initiate the hip action necessary to get the legs around. The push is a combination of elbow extension and horizontal flexion. Hence, this exercise is valuable training for effective execution of the combination.

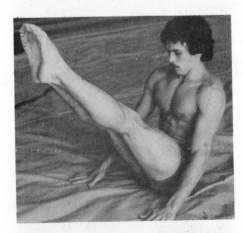

6 Back and Shoulder Developer

This exercise is designed to strengthen the muscles of the posterior aspect of the forearm, arm, shoulder, and back. The forearm extensors (1) control the position of the weight and grip on, for example, the parallel bars or the rings. The elbow extensor (2) is strengthened as it contracts to keep the arm straight. This muscle, as well as the posterior deltoid (3), aids in proper positioning of the upper extremity, since part of the elbow

extensor and all of the posterior deltoid crosses the shoulder joint. The posterior deltoid originates from the spine of the scapula. Thus to prevent excessive lateral movement of this bone, the rhomboids (4) contract to stabilize it. These muscles are used during the upward thrust of the arms when performing a *back salto*. They are also used when performing swinging movements that require the body to be pushed out in front of the base—the hands—particularly when swinging on the parallel bars.

7 Bent-Knee Abdominal Sit-Up

A student with weak abdominal muscles should be encouraged to engage in this exercise. With the knees and hips flexed, the rectus abdominis (1) becomes the prime mover for hip flexion. Hence, this muscle will become stronger. Since the long head of the rectus femoris (one of the four

quadriceps) passes the hip joint, it too aids hip flexion. The hamstrings (3) contract to maintain proper knee flexion during the curling phase of the exercise. The tibialis anterior and other extensor muscles of the leg (4) aid in dorsal flexion of the feet. Naturally, the feet must be maintained as in the figure to keep the body positioned properly.

8 V Seat.

Although the photo may lead the reader to interpret this exercise as an isometric type, it is actually very dynamic, with the legs moving up and down. In this way, the hip flexors and the trunk flexors will get stronger. To reduce resistance to the upward mo-

tion (or hip flexion), the hamstrings should be adequately stretched. (See stretches later in chapter.) The knees are kept straight due to the contraction of the quadriceps. The feet are pointed (or plantar-flexed) due to the pull of the tendons arising from the muscles of the posterior-medial aspect of the leg.

9 Push-ups

The arms and shoulders of young performers often are very weak. Lack of upper extremity strength hinders the acquisition of most gymnastic skills. This is one obvious reason that teachers and coaches stress exercises such as push-ups. It can be used both as a warm-up and as a strength devel-

oper. The muscles responsible for the downward and upward motions of a push-up are the triceps brachii and the shoulder flexors. There are situations in which too many push-ups may be detrimental to the student. For example, if a student is round-shouldered, such an exercise can make the condition worse by shortening the pectoral muscles.

10 Sit-up Variations

While the young girl is performing a bent-knee sit-up in which the feet are allowed to come off the floor, the young boy increases the resistance by keeping his legs straight. Both types are very beneficial and necessary for a well-organized training program. Again, these exercises increase the strength of the hip and trunk flexors. These make it easier to perform tuck or pike flips, and other moves requiring hip flexion or controlled pelvic alignment for proper execution.

Flexibility

Flexibility is defined as the ability to move passively through a desired range of motion about a joint. Flexibility training:

- reduces the possibility of injury
- enhances muscular action with minimal resistance to the tissues
- contributes to perfection of movement

A student or gymnast who is flexible is less prone to injury since he can adapt quickly to a given situation. When a muscle cannot respond quickly with minimum resistance, the tissues about a joint become susceptible to injury. Resistance resulting from lack of suppleness wastes considerable energy, even when attempting basic skills. Hence, an increased range of motion allows for more efficient execution.

The solution to poor flexibility is simply progressive and systematic training. Stretching procedures are usually based on one of two approaches. The first and perhaps more traditional one is the *ballistic* (or bobbing) stretch, in which the performer uses the body's momentum to extend the muscles and collagenous tissues surrounding specific joints. The second approach is called the slow or *static* stretch. It involves a controlled body movement, in which a certain position is held for a few seconds. Although both methods appear beneficial, the latter is more common, since the performer is less susceptible to injury to the tissues.

The main point is that, as with strength building, one must be systematic and progressive to achieve a greater range of motion about specific joints. Select an exercise and work at it every day. The following are good exercises to increase flexibility.

1 Back and Leg Stretch

The muscles at the back of the thigh, the buttocks, and the lower back area must be reasonably flexible to allow for various gymnastic movements. While one gymnast has the arms above her shoulders, the other is fully flexed at the hips to allow the chest area to contact the legs. The latter position is not possible without excellent flexibility. If you are able to stretch forward as in this position, more gymnastic moves are possible. For example, without adequate flexibility both gymnasts would find it very difficult to raise their legs very high when performing a back walkover. The increased range of motion about the hip and lower back area allows for easier displacement of the performer's center of gravity behind the base when beginning the back walkover. This is just one advantage of increased range of motion.

2 Back and Leg Stretch (Dorsi-Flexed)

The gymnast on the right has her feet pointed (or *plantar-flexed*), while the gymnast on the left is pointing her feet up and back toward the head (or *dorsi-flexed*). The first exercise is the general approach for the hamstring stretch. The second is useful, how-ever, especially when one wants to stretch the muscles of the posterior aspect of the leg (i.e., from the knee to the foot). The second approach allows for more progressive stretching throughout the lower extremity.

3 Hurdler's Stretch

This is a common exercise used in a number of different sports, such as volleyball and track events. The exercise is designed to stretch the hamstrings and adductors on the straight leg side. It appears that the bent knee position of the second leg allows for easier forward stretch of the straight leg. Assuming that this is true, the increased motion will allow for greater flexibility. The only problem related to this stretch is that unnecessary strain may be placed on the medial collateral ligament of the bent knee. This is particularly the case when the athlete changes from one side to the other while stretching. Moving the upper body to a vertical position and over on the bent knee side places considerable stress on the medial side of the knee joint.

4 Adductor (Medial Thigh) Stretch

With the feet placed in close to each other as noted in the photo, the inside muscles of the thigh (the adductor muscles) are stretched. The closer the feet to the body and the wider the knees, the more the muscles are stretched. If the performer leans forward, other muscles are stretched. The main purpose of this exercise is to stretch the adductor muscles, and allow for better *abduction* of the lower extremity.*

*Abduction refers to raising the leg away from the midline of the body.

5 Adductor and Hamstring Stretch

The adductor and hamstring muscles can be stretched by spreading the legs as wide as possible. Since this type of motion is necessary in men's and women's gymnastics, it is very productive to practice a progressive approach to this exercise. At first, to avoid too much muscle soreness, the legs should not be placed too far apart. Later, after realizing some increase in range of motion, the legs should be spread further. The thigh muscles, as well as the muscles of the hip, will gradually adapt to the increase in resistance.

6 Straddle Hamstring Stretch

This exercise is like the hurdler's stretch, except that both legs are straight. The gymnast should first stretch on one side and then move to the other. The downward motion should be controlled and held for a few seconds before moving on to the other side. Note that the performer's chest is placed directly over the stretched leg. The hands should be positioned as far as possible beyond the pointed foot.

7 Straddle Hamstring Stretch (Shoulder Inside)

The only difference between this exercise and the one previously mentioned is that the shoulder is placed inside the performer's knee. This added increase in forward lean produces greater resistance; this allows for increased adaptation of the posterior-medial thigh muscles.

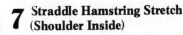

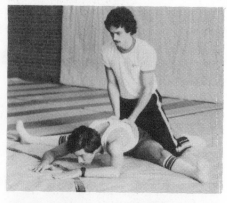

8 Hamstring and Lower Back Stretch (Using a Partner)

Note the pressure that the partner is placing on the performer's lower back. This aids in the necessary downward movement of the abdomen. But when the downward pressure is excessive, there is a sensation of pain along the medial aspect of the knee. The performer's feet are dorsi-flexed, thus stretching the muscles of the posterior aspect of the leg. This is also a good approach to help the performer keep the back straight when moving forward.

9 Hip Flexor Stretch

By flexing at the hip and the knee, and then pulling the extremity over the chest, the performer applies the necessary tension to create an increased range of motion in the hip flexor of the straight leg side. Gymnasts, like the one in the foreground, with an unusually wide range of motion in the leg that moves over the chest, can keep the leg straight and stretch it as well as the hip flexor on the remaining straight leg side. If the left leg (or straight leg) of both performers was flexed at the knee or hip, one might assume that the hip flexor on that side was tight. The extreme position of the performer in the foreground, with the leg positioned closer to the face, should not be attempted until there has been adequate practice.

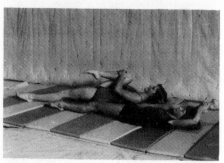

10 Hip Flexor Stretch to Splits

This is an exercise that allows for increased hip flexibility. At first, the performer should assume the semi-standing position, in which a small motion aids in stretching the hip flexor on the left or straight leg side. As the exercise progresses, the right foot is moved further from the performer's hips. The hip flexors become more stretched until one gradually assumes the full splits position. (See performer at right.) Note that the side split requires an increased range of motion in the hip flexors of the back leg and adductor, and hamstring flexibility in the front leg. Hence, a combination of specific exercises is often necessary to create the desired thigh and hip suppleness.

11 Bridge Up Variations

Depending on the type of bridge up used, one will get completely different effects. For example, the performer on the top is stretching the shoulder joints and the upper thoracic spine more than the lower back. By extending the legs, as noted in the photograph, the performer is able to place more stress on the shoulder joints. The gradual increase in shoulder joint flexibility allows for more vertical positioning of the arms, an advantage with respect to such skills as the back or front walkover.

The second type of bridge up is performed by the gymnast on the bottom. She is pushing her stomach up vertically, which stretches the lower back more than other aspects of the back and shoulders. The arms are not as vertical as those of the gymnast on the left; nor are the legs together and straight. These are distinct skills, with completely different outcomes.

Consider, for example, a young girl with ample lower back suppleness reaching back and placing her hands on the mat. However, as the student contacts the mat, the teacher notices that the arms are diagonally positioned. In effect, the shoulders are very tight. The obvious exercise for the young girl would be the one on the left, since it stretches the shoulder joints.

12 **Lower Back and Gluteal Stretch**

The beginning point for this exercise is with the legs completely extended above the performer's hips. (See performer in background.) As the legs are lowered, the feet are positioned beyond the head. The legs can be kept straight or flexed. The straight leg position places more stretch on the hamstring, gluteal, and lower back muscles. While the bent-knee position often relaxes the hamstrings, the

gluteal and lower back muscles continue to be stretched.

13 **Spinal Column Stretch**

This is a good exercise to stretch the shoulders, as noted in the gymnast on the left. The usual approach is to stretch first the left shoulder and then the right, followed by both. (See both gymnasts in the figure.) Then, the gymnast is instructed to place one arm

under the chest as demonstrated by the performer on the right. When done correctly, the thoracic and lumbar vertebrae, and associated ligaments and muscles, will be stretched first on one side and then the other as one arm and then the other is placed under the chest.

14 **Anterior Chest and Shoulder Stretch**

With the help of a partner, the performer's arms are raised above the shoulders in what is referred to as a hyperflexed position. By maintaining some muscular tension about the shoulders, the partner is able to adjust the position of the raised arms so that it enhances upper back suppleness, as well as the anterior chest wall. This exercise is really no more than the bridge up done with the legs straight,

except that the head is not *cervically hyperextended.**

**Cervically hyperextended* means that the head is tilted back and upward, as when looking at the stars.

15 **Pectoral and Shoulder Stretch (Arms Horizontally Positioned)**

Note that the partner has her left knee positioned at the midpoint of the performer's back to aid in applying tension to the anterior chest wall and the shoulder muscles. This type of an exercise is especially important when one is ready to learn, for example, the eagle catch on the uneven parallel bars.

16 Pectoral and Shoulder Stretch (Arms Vertically Positioned)

The performer is in a sitting position, with the legs straight and feet pointed. The arms are hyperflexed, with the partner gradually increasing presure about the shoulders. Both men and women should practice this exercise to increase shoulder flexibility.

17 Pectoral and Shoulder Stretch (Bent-Arm Position)

By flexing at the elbows, the partner can help apply more force about the shoulder and upper trunk to increase the range of motion in these areas. This position of the arms in this exercise allows for an additional range of motion that is not realized in the previously mentioned exercises.

18 Lower Back and Hamstring Stretch Variations

Note that the gymnast on the left has her chest positioned very close to her thighs. This places an equal amount of stress on both legs and the lower back. Also, by placing the hands behind the feet, additional resistance may be encountered. Some students prefer to stretch predominantly one leg and then the other, as noted in the case of the gymnast on the right. The latter approach is probably not as stressful as the first.

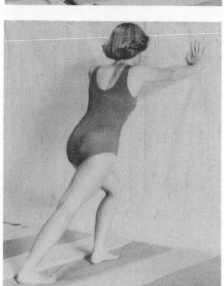

19 Achilles Tendon Stretch

By moving the right foot back, while still keeping it on the mat, the performer is able to apply sufficient stress to the Achilles tendon and the muscles at the posterior of the leg. This exercise is extremely useful in preventing the rather common rupture of the Achilles tendon (that is, the tendon of the gastrocnemius and soleus). They both come together and insert on the calcaneus or heel bone of the foot.

20 Hamstring and Hip Flexor Stretch (With a Partner)

With the student's back against the wall as a support, the partner raises the leg to a point where resistance is encountered. In the illustration, the performer's right leg is raised, resulting in stretching of the hamstrings. The support leg is stretched as well, particularly the hip flexors.

21 Hamstring and Adductor Stretch Variation

Note that the bar is positioned at a height to create the desired stretch of the performer's left leg. The hamstrings of the left leg are being stretched as the performer leans forward on the anterior aspect of the raised leg. Through the use of the hands, additional pressure can be applied to move the chest closer to the leg. Positioning the support leg further from the bar creates even more pressure. Note that the support leg is positioned in such a way that it stretches the adductors (the muscles on the medial side of the thigh). So, the exercise is useful in increasing adductor flexibility. By placing the foot of the support leg closer to the bar, the stress is shifted more to the hip flexors than the adductors.

22 Adductor Stretch (Medial Thigh)

This exercise can be very useful in helping the student adjust to such skills as the forward roll straddle rise, or the straddle jump on the trampoline. It represents a different approach to stretching the medial aspect of the thigh. Since these muscles are basically very tight, the partner must take her time and apply pressure slowly to the raised leg. Both legs must be stretched.

23 Anterior Thigh and Low Abdominal Stretch (With a Partner)

This is an extremely useful exercise for increasing the performer's ability to raise the leg. With the left leg raised, the anterior aspect of the thigh (i.e., the quadriceps and the hip flexors) is stretched. While gradually increasing extension of the lower back, the lower portion of the abdominal area is also stretched. Again, both legs should be stretched very gradually and systematically. The raised leg should be kept as straight as possible when pressure is applied.

Additional Relaxation Techniques

In summary, several stretching procedures are suggested for additional discussion and use by the student or athlete. A warm to fairly hot shower can be helpful in reducing tenseness in the lower back after practice. Regular stretching in the shower enhances the range of motion in tight areas that need special care. For example, should a student have difficulty hyperflexing the arm (i.e., raising the arm above the shoulders), a hot shower will allow the tight area to be stretched without the tension often felt when heat is not used.

Some coaches have also substituted using ice for heat as a way to relax muscles. Although it may be somewhat uncomfortable at first, it is a useful technique, and will result in increased suppleness. If the performer feels any pain after practice, ice is recommended.

Concentrating on relaxing specific muscles has also proven useful, especially for students of yoga. Without a doubt, gymnastics students can also benefit from this technique. It must be practiced regularly, and over a fairly long period of time. It is conceivable that students and athletes can benefit from attempts to relax the specific muscles involved in a given skill or sequence. By thinking through the skill, it is possible that less energy may be needed for a given physical task. In this way, the student is encouraged to be highly selective in the use of the muscles related to performance.

Coordination

The ability to execute skills in a coordinated manner often divides the student from the gymnast. The student is more concerned with merely getting through the basic mechanics of a cartwheel, and doesn't usually concern himself with fundamentals. A young girls asked to perform a handstand thinks about the act of performing and the possibility of failure. The gymnast, on the other hand, acknowledges the step-by-step mechanics of the skills. Moreover, the gymnast has the ability to make appropriate transitions, such as a forward roll single-leg rise to a handstand, or a forward roll single-leg rise into a cartwheel with a one-half turn into a handstand front limber to stand. Although these are basic types of transitions, the performance of these skills goes beyond mere recognition of correct performance. The gymnast, in essence, learns a sense of pace, and achieves confidence in his ability to perform in a relaxed manner. Therefore, the finished look is more economical and worth emulating.

Put another way, a coordinated performance is a proper interplay between the desired and the necessary involvement of specific muscles to achieve a particular objective, and the apparent lack of noticeable contraction or interference of unnecessary muscle tension. Obviously, coordinated performances do not occur easily. In fact, to become coordinated at a given task, it is essential that the performer practice movements specific to a given skill or sequence.

A major factor that detracts from the ability to coordinate a short sequence of skills is the excessive tension in the muscles. Unnecessary tension and muscle tightness limit the flexibility of the performer. Jacobson's relaxation-training approach will help in learning how to contract and then relax specific muscle groups. This method is useful before, and possibly after, a performance. However, the ability to relax while in motion requires a high degree of mental concentration on body tension. One must be able to define in her own mind the desired level of muscular tension relative to a given skill. This process is very difficult. Thus several basic blueprints for achieving successful relaxation are outlined for the reader's evaluation and use. Jacobson's approach follows.

Have the students or athletes practice relaxing by lying on their backs. Mats or some soft surface should be used. The room should be fairly quiet with minimum lighting. Music may also be helpful in achieving a relaxed atmosphere.

The teacher or coach, speaking in a low voice, should suggest relaxation exercises for the following areas of the body: (1) hips and abdomen, (2) feet and legs, (3) chest and arms, and (4) face and neck muscles. The leader should instruct the performers, for instance, to contract the thighs while leaving the rest of the body as relaxed as possible, and then gradually relax the thighs. The contraction should be for at least thirty seconds. The relaxation phase should be at least as long. The order of progression is generally from the feet to the legs and upward. As the students learn to relax specific muscles, they should be instructed to relate these muscles to the specifics of given skills. This approach may help students realize some of their muscles are contracted, even when they fail to perceive the increased tension. Learning when and how to dissipate unnecessary muscular tension is the key to coordinated movements.

Students and athletes should be encouraged to picture themselves moving through the skill or routine, and at the same time tense the muscles most involved in the skill. They should be instructed to relax and, again, allow the mental process to evaluate the body movements. Although this approach to neuro-muscular training is somewhat confusing, it can become a valuable part of the teaching/coaching process.

To move with ease and grace, the performer must train mentally, as well as physically.

PART 2

SPOTTING IN CLASSROOM SITUATIONS

3
Class Organization

Class organization is the key to a safe and effective program. Without prior planning, a gymnastics class can degenerate into a circle of events and emotions. To avoid problems and to create an atmosphere for creative learning, the instructor must be organized. This is especially true when there is a large number of students. Here, we are dealing with students in sixth grade (twelve years old) and older. If two spotters are used, anyone at that age can help the teacher. Since gymnastics requires assistance for performances, a major part of the organizational process is identifying competent instructors to assist the teacher. Since there are few qualified spotters, the teacher is forced to train the most qualified students to assist in teaching specific skills.

It is necessary for the teacher to provide instruction in spotting techniques, as well as the more traditional descriptive analysis of gymnastic skills. This particular approach, however, is not easy to implement. It requires considerable patience, planning, and hard work. The following suggestions, if used correctly and with proper anticipation, should prove useful in reducing the stress the teacher often experiences the first few class periods.

Fundamentals of Good Teaching

Knowledge of the teaching area. The gymnastics teacher must study such things as the type and arrangement of equipment, placement of mats, lighting, ventilation, and medical procedures. These factors must be analyzed for their influence on individual students and the class. Unfortunately, too many teachers wait until the class is under way before making changes in mat placement or other factors that should be handled before class. The type and placement of equipment have a tremendous bearing on the natural flow of the class. It should be determined before the start of class whether there is adequate lighting to avoid unnecessary ankle sprains and other accidents.

Equipment. When the class begins tumbling, the mats should abut each other the full length of the expected tumbling area. Most teachers do not find it necessary to place mats around the trampoline. If the class is given proper directions for getting on and off the trampoline, contact with the floor can be controlled. Spotting and frame pads are, however, important for trampoline skills.

Mats of at least one inch thickness are essential for apparatus work. Depending on the difficulty of particular skills (especially during dismounts), mats of six to eight inches of foam padding may be necessary. These mats are generally known as crash pads. As a general rule, mats should be placed anywhere a performer is likely to fall, or where an uncontrolled performer may contact an immovable object. On the uneven parallel bars, for example, mats should be placed under the bars, as well as on the dismount side of the apparatus. To avoid uneven surfaces, mats should never be overlapped. Finally, special care should be taken to prevent students from damaging the mats by folding them improperly. The Nissen mat is especially expensive, and should be folded on top of itself in sections of two prior to moving it or using it as an aid for reaching a performer.

Warm-up exercises. When the students enter the gymnastics room, they should be instructed in warm-up exercises specific to gymnastics. These exercises should progressively increase joint flexibility and muscle tone. The warm-up period should be at least four to eight minutes, but the most important thing is that the major joints are stretched. This part of the class also provides the instructor with an opportunity to examine quickly the caliber of student enrolled in the class. The instructor should observe, for example, whether some of the students are overweight or very inflexible. This type of information can help the teacher plan for these students, and any problem areas that may distract from a safe gymnastics program.

Progressive tumbling skills. Most teachers find it beneficial to get the class immediately involved in light to gradually more intense tumbling skills and transitions. The warm-up helps to stretch out the muscles, and the tumbling helps to keep the performer's body temperature raised. Both are necessary for good body flexibility. Also, involving the class in a common objective aids reluctant students in overcoming uneasiness.

Another advantage is that tumbling skills can be taught to a large number of students. Depending on the way in which the mats are arranged, almost all the students can participate at once. Skills such as head- and handstands, scales, and other relatively static moves can be practiced across the mat. Those students not performing can aid as spotters.

Later, after the students have acquired some of the fundamentals of certain skills, the mats should be extended to keep interest high. For example, most students find it challenging to perform combinations such as: forward roll, jump stretch, forward roll; or forward roll, single-leg rise, two-arm cartwheel, turn, handstand, forward roll. This is preferable to having students repeat forward rolls over and over. Performing relatively easy tumbling skills in combination adds interest and challenge to a gymnastics class.

Organize the class into groups. Following the tumbling session, most teachers find it advantageous to quickly divide the class into small groups (each with a leader) to work on specific skills on the parallel bars, high bar, rings, beam, and horse, to mention a few. This approach allows the students more exposure time per event. It also helps get the students involved with each other in a teaching-learning situation. It is important that the students communicate well within each group, and that the teacher properly supervises all groups. If a group begins to play around, the teacher should immediately step in and encourage a safer approach.

Explain and demonstrate the skill. The teacher is responsible for explaining and demonstrating the fundamentals of each skill expected of the students. If the teacher cannot demonstrate the skills, she must be able to find someone in class who can perform them, or demonstrate the correct spotting technique with a student who can come close to performing the skills by herself. This approach must be used with each new apparatus and all new skills. The teacher should not assume that the students can perform the skills safely. If any assumption is made, it should be that the students cannot initially perform the skills safely by themselves. The instructor should expect to spot everything until the skills are fully learned. The teacher must discuss the mechanics of safe spotting in adjunct with a descriptive analysis of the skill. It is the teacher's responsibility to assist student leaders in acquiring the correct spotting techniques specific to the skills at a given apparatus.

Encourage student responsibility. Students should learn to be responsible for their actions. It is the teacher's responsibility to communicate this to the students. If a student acts in a manner that is harmful to himself and possibly the class, then he must not be allowed to participate until his attitude changes. Students must show good judgment relative to skill progression as well. Difficult skills must not be attempted until the proper time and with adequate spotting. Students must come to understand the importance of proper mat placement and management of equipment. The student is ultimately responsible for acquiring essential conditioning factors, such as muscle endurance and strength. Lastly, students need to understand that they are responsible for the safety of each other. They must learn not only how to perform gymnastic skills, but also to spot each other.

Have clear and realistic objectives. The instructor in gymnastics, as in any sport, must have definite objectives. In order to provide both an understandable and a safe program or class, they must be clear and realistic. The presentation of the skills for each event must be progressive in its approach, yet in accordance with the students' abilities and needs. If students fail to see the meaning of certain skills, especially the more difficult ones, then the interest level is often less than desired.

The teacher must be consistent in the way the class is handled. Joking around during one class period followed by a more demanding attitude in the next will only create unnecessary problems, with negative influences on the learning of gymnastic skills. The instructor's attitude must be realistic. He should be optimistic and patient, allowing the slow student to progress safely and meaningfully. The instructor must also be able to discern between the student who is ready to perform and the one who still needs special help.

Since most gymnastic classes are designed for beginners, it is probably safer and wiser to aim the class at the beginner. Never set the class objectives around a few semiadvanced performers. Such an approach will only set the stage for increased injury and loss of interest for the beginners. It is the teacher's responsibility to determine the performance level of her students; she should never accept the students' comments as the final word. In this way, she determines for herself when the students are ready for more advanced skills. The instructor, not the students, directs the class. Due to its inherent potential for injury to the performer, this must always be the case in gymnastics.

After the students have practiced for ten to fifteen minutes at a given event, they should rotate to the next apparatus. The number of stations per class depends on the length of the class, the number of skills to be learned at each station, and the number of students assigned to each station.

As the class comes to a close, all students should be brought together for three to five minutes of mild stretching. At this time, the teacher has an opportunity to speak to all members and share such comments as, "everybody did an excellent job today" or "the spotting was not as good as it has been." These few minutes together help summarize the class and provide direction for the next class.

Additional Organizational Considerations

When moving from floor work to apparatus work, it becomes increasingly difficult to keep all the students involved at a given apparatus. The obvious reason is that all the students cannot use, for example, one set of uneven parallel bars, while five to six tumbling mats can keep the entire class very active. Therefore, it seems necessary to present some possibilities for dealing with this problem. Remember, however, when teaching men, women, or both, that events specific to each should be explored for positive teaching results. While men can aid women in executing their skills, the reverse is generally not the case. Due to the dynamic nature of most men's skills, women do not generally have the strength to compensate for poor performances. So, while men can spot for both men's and

women's events, women should not be allowed to swing on the rings or to spot men on the rings, unless assisted by another person. Women can, however, spot effectively for beginner's skills, such as those on the parallel bars.

Uneven parallel bars. To get more students involved on the bars:

1. The teacher can modify the men's parallel bars to just one bar, which acts as a low bar for girls. This is an excellent approach for introducing beginning and intermediate skills that require only one bar for proper execution.

2. Students can use the men's high bar as a low bar. The main objective here is to provide an opportunity for as many girls as possible to participate. By lowering the high bar, girls can work those skills normally learned on the low bar of the women's uneven parallel bars.

3. Several girls can be taught on one bar (with a spotter for each girl). This is an excellent method of increasing participation, but it is usually used only with young girls. Use of a single bar requires that the performers be well separated from each other. The spotters (one per performer) should stand behind the performers, regardless of the sides the performers are on. In this way, the performers will be positioned between the spotters.

Balance beam. Though most schools already have a balance beam, several beams are better than one. To get the entire class involved with beam work, the teacher could:

1. have the school workshop build four to five small beams, varying in length and height as necessary

2. place a tape on the floor to serve as a straight line for beam work

Students should understand that beam skills are for the most part acquired on the floor prior to performing them on the beam. Initially, the beam should be positioned only a few inches from the mat. Later, after the skills are fully learned, they can be attempted on the large beam. When this transition occurs, however, the skill should always be done with a spotter until it becomes automatic.

Vaulting. When using the vaulting horse, the following suggestions may prove useful. While ten or so students are using the side horse for vaulting, others can use an alternate apparatus (perhaps built by the school or simply boxes placed on one another. Ten more may use the trampoline to vault on, especially with such vaults as the squat, straddle, stoop, etc. Ten others may use a Mini-Tramp with appropriate mats. The point is that with some imagination all the students can be provided an opportunity to perform.

Trampoline and gymnastics equipment. Most schools are limited in this area, due either to the cost of the apparatus or more likely the inherent danger associated with trampoline work. For those schools providing trampoline work, it is not a safe practice to substitute homemade equipment for professional quality equipment. A type of trampoline that does not fold up, which some smaller companies are now sell-ing, can be useful if used correctly. This type of trampoline, which is usually round, is potentially beneficial with young children. Children seem to like it, and it is less expensive than the folding type. All trampolines must have adequate mats around the top for proper absorption.

It is also unwise to substitute homemade equipment for men's parallel bars, high bar, side horse, or rings. The workmanship that goes into the making of these pieces of equipment is very high. Anything less, unless built by a competent craftsman and gymnast, may prove dangerous.

4

Class Spotting Procedures

It is imperative that instructors teach the fundamentals of good spotting, due to the increased interest in gymnastics, as well as liability factors. Help from the students provides the teacher with additional opportunity to analyze student performances. Moreover, this ensures a safer atmosphere for learning gymnastics skills. Students thus become an integral part of the teaching process. They must come to realize the progressive nature of gymnastics: spotting can be viewed as a continuum from merely touching a performer to a more demanding involvement, in which the spotter protects and guides the performer to avoid a potentially dangerous situation. In most cases, however, the spotter needs to provide verbal encouragement, as well as a certain amount of physical help. This type of help is generally referred to as a *light spot*.* A *heavy spot* occurs when a performer is totally unable to perform a given skill, thus making the performer dependent on the spotter to avoid injury.

When teaching students how to spot each other, the teacher should be sure that students:

- know the basic components of the skills
- know the importance of anticipating dangerous situations during the execution of a skill
- understand the biomechanical aspects of spotting

- are sensitive to the performer's needs and weaknesses
- are aware of the necessity for verbal correction and feedback

Essentials for Developing as a Spotter

In addition to the material already presented, there are at least four essentials for developing as a spotter. These factors are presented in the order they should be analyzed.

Demonstrating the spotting technique. The spotting technique must be demonstrated in class by the teacher or some other competent person. The students should become aware of the components of the entire spotting process. The student spotters must be given specific directions, with special emphasis on the more difficult aspects of the technique or skill. Students should be encouraged to ask questions for clarification.

Analyzing the spotting technique. The teacher must emphasize the elements of particular techniques. For example, if the students are asked to spot a back roll to the handstand position, then the teacher should point out the following elements. The spotter should stand approximately an arm length from the performer to insure a close spot. Hand contact with the performer's back helps the performer sit correctly instead of falling backward to the floor. As the performer sits and tucks to begin the roll, the spotter

---

*A *light spot* refers to a spotting technique with minimum physical assistance to aid the performer in putting the finishing touches on a given performance. This may include verbal encouragement.

should provide an upward thrust to the thighs to aid the performer during arm extension. At this point the spotter should be standing with one foot on each side of the performer's hands. As the handstand position is realized, the spotter should encourage a straight handstand position. Finally, a hand should be placed at the performer's waist to control the descent to the floor. These concerns represent some of the more important aspects of the spotting process. Analysis of each skill is a critical part of learning spotting techniques.

Repetition of the spotting technique. The spotter must repeatedly practice the technique for spotting a skill, just as he would for learning the skill being spotted. The teacher should emphasize the spotter's movement toward the performer, the initial hand contact, and the follow-through every time the spotter practices the technique. In essence, the technique must be repeated until it becomes an automatic response. Repetition is necessary for acquiring the quickness and insight needed to become a competent spotter. At this time, the teacher must correct any bad habits that are developing. Taking a few minutes to keep the spotting technique acceptable may actually prevent an injury.

Supervising the spotting technique. To ensure that the spotters are developing correctly, the teacher must supervise the spotting process. The spotter must continually adapt until the right technique has been perfected. During this transition the spotter must realize there is no room for carelessness, so the performer is assured of a responsible person to help him.

As soon as the performer begins to demonstrate an ability to accept responsibility for a correct and safe performance, the spotter should gradually reduce assistance. Eventually the assistance should be no more than a readiness to help the performer. This decision, however, is the responsibility of the teacher. In this way, spotters help extend the teacher's control over the class. In situations where all the students are both performers and spotters, the class should be a safe one for all concerned.

Depending on the age and spotting experience of the students, the teacher may want to use two spotters (one on each side of the performer) to ensure that the performer is properly aided. Two spotters provide more total strength and, hence, better control over the performer. But the spotters must learn to work together. As the performer demonstrates his ability to adjust to the mechanics of the skill, one spotter may step back, allowing the second to spot the performer. As one spotter continues to spot, the other then concentrates on how well the performer is acquiring the skill. Spotters can alternate with each other to avoid becoming overly exhausted. This approach helps develop excellent spotting techniques, as well as safe performances. The student learns both how to spot and how to perform.

Student Spotters

Unfortunately, too few teachers have used students as spotters in their classes. This appears to stem from the more traditional emphasis on descriptive aspects of gymnastic skills. This approach, however, has proven to be lacking, especially in the area of safety. It is one thing to describe a skill, and yet another to learn to perform it. Good performance depends on someone else being able to correct any deficiencies. A spotter thus helps insure safety.

The teacher's role when presenting new skills is to describe the spotter's movements, as well as the basics of the skill. Student spotters can free the teacher from having to assist every student in the class. This alone will help keep the teacher from being physically overworked. This allows the teacher to work individually with students having special problems. Educating students in spotting will improve their understanding of the teacher's role.

In summary, student spotters will help the teacher work with students who are unable to perform without some manual assistance from a friend, teacher, or coach. Progressive spotting provides students with the opportunity to at least feel what it is like to move through, for example, a valdez or a back handspring. This is also a vital part of every gymnastics class or program. We must always be concerned for every person who wants to learn gymnastics, whether strong, weak, flexible, or whatever.

5

Safety Factors in Spotting

The teacher or coach must examine the gymnastics area prior to each teaching or training session. It may be necessary, for example, to remove certain equipment such as excess mats or improperly folded mats to help prevent injuries. Apparatus such as the uneven parallel bars and the balance beam should always be checked for proper stability and alignment. To prevent the twisting of ankles, beam and bars should be checked for placement of mats so there are no gaps or overlaps. Both men's and women's bars and the beam should be checked for cracking and splitting. The high bar should be checked regularly for accumulation of chalk.

The point is that all the equipment should be checked for possible damage or other conditions that may hinder or hurt the performer. It is the instructor's responsibility to monitor these throughout the program or class. But students, too, must learn to inspect the equipment and check for proper placement of mats.

Students are also responsible for their physical and emotional condition when participating in gymnastics. They should be aware that their physical condition has tremendous bearing on their safety. A progressive warm-up and a systematic approach to strength training prior to working on the apparatus go a long way toward preventing injuries. For instance, the performer has an increased ability to recover from a fall by using an appropriate follow-up, such as a forward roll. An extra reserve of muscle strength and endurance will help ensure a safe recovery, thus decreasing

the chances of injury. The better conditioned the performers, the easier they are to spot. This is one reason why coaches oftentimes have it easier than instructors who teach only beginners.

Performers need to wear the proper clothing when working out. In addition, all jewelry must be removed to avoid complications such as fractures of the small bones of the fingers. Participants must not be allowed to chew gum. The gum may become lodged in the respiratory passages and prevent adequate respiration.

Adequate rest periods should always follow strenuous workouts. The duration of the rest periods will depend on the physical condition of the participants and the intensity of the training or teaching session. When possible, after a strenuous workout the skills should be varied, with more emphasis on transitional and less physically demanding skills.

As part of the conditioning and teaching process, students should become aware of the influence of negative attitudes on performance potential. Mental attitude can make the difference between success and failure, and can affect the likelihood of injury. This fundamental principle must permeate teaching and coaching. Teachers can help by encouraging students both to think positively and to give themselves a fair chance to learn gymnastics. A positive attitude will help maintain safety in this sport.

When it is evident that a person is extremely reluctant to perform, the teacher should take the initiative to help smooth out the problem. It may become necessary to meet with the student in a room separate from the workout area prior to or after class to discuss the problem. The main thing is to not overlook this aspect of teaching/coaching, and if at all possible to do something constructive about it.

The following general safety precautions are outlined for: tumbling, balance beam, uneven parallel bars, vaulting, trampoline, parallel bars, high bar, side horse, rings, and Mini-Tramp. These major points should help direct the students, teachers, and the class in general. The concerned teacher/coach will no doubt be able to identify many other items of interest.

Tumbling

Make sure that the mats are properly placed and connected. Place them in such a way that performers will not contact the wall or an apparatus. Always use mats of sufficient thickness and number to accommodate the class.

Learn to anticipate problems with skills requiring either a run or good flexibility. When force is introduced into the picture, the student must be able to use it to advantage.

Do not allow the students to progress to the harder skills, such as the back walkover or the front handspring, until easier skills like the back or the front limber have been mastered. (See the Saddle Stretch and the Adductor Stretch in chapter 2.) The basics must be constantly stressed to both beginners and advanced performers. Students should be encouraged to work on combinations, rather than one skill of great difficulty.

It is important to teach the spotters how to perform without making mistakes. They must learn how to spot, just as the tumbler must learn how to tumble. Both the spotter and the tumbler require considerable practice to become good, consistent performers. Be sure to spot any skills that may result in twisted ankles.

Balance Beam

When more than one beam is used in a small area, make sure performers are far enough apart to avoid hitting each other when dismounting. In addition, keep the beams away from doors, bleachers, and gymnastics equipment.

Students should be instructed not to get on the beam until the teacher is present to supervise. Even experienced performers should ask for supervision when attempting new or advanced skills. A spotter should be present for all skills requiring assistance for safe and effective execution. The instructor is respon-

sible for teaching the correct mechanics for various spotting techniques.

Although some performers prefer to be barefoot when working the beam, others feel more comfortable wearing tight-fitting socks or gymnastics shoes to enhance contact and balance. The method chosen is up to the performer and her coach, and depends on the performer's training experience.

When students begin to lose their balance, they must sometimes give in to the unstable condition. There is a fine line between knowing when to fight to maintain balance and when one should simply dismount.

Mats should be placed on both sides and at the ends of the beam. When attempting skills such as a forward roll or a cartwheel (with or without a spotter), it is a good idea to place a crash mat under the beam for extra protection.

When dismounting, be sure to avoid the supports. If a dismount involves the arms, the elbows must be straight and the shoulders must be over the hands when leaving the beam. When the performer makes contact with the mat on landing, he should flex at the hips and knees to reduce the force of impact.

To avoid landing on a sharp edge of the *beat board*, it must be removed as the mount is made.* This is generally done by the spotter.

In all beginning skills, such as walks, hops, and dips, the spotter should walk along the beam with a hand held up in case the performer needs it for balance.

When the performer is ready to attempt the skill without a spotter, the teacher should be present and alert for any problems. Telling the student that she is ready to perform by herself is always difficult. One can only hope that the instructor's judgment is right. Again, the spotter must stand to the side of the beam and the performer, alert and ready to respond to any faults that require assistance to avoid injury.

Uneven Parallel Bars

It is natural that much of the safety information presented for the beam applies to the bars as well. The teacher/coach should also be sure of the following before each class or practice:

- Has the equipment been checked?
- Is there an adequate number of mats, and are they properly positioned?

---

*A *beat board* is a short, inclined board used for takeoffs in vaulting, and when mounting the beam or the bars.

- Is the beat board or any object, such as low parallel bars, extra mats, shoes, etc., placed dangerously close to an apparatus, so it may cause an accident?
- Are there sufficient spotters for the new skills?
- Are spotters correctly positioned to aid the performer?
- Are the hand contact points between spotter and performer correct?
- Are the spotters emotionally prepared to spot the difficult skills?
- Are the performers physically ready to attempt the intermediate and advanced skills?
- Do the performers understand the mechanics of the more difficult skills?

Vaulting

Students should wear some kind of shoe to prevent excessive shock to the metatarsal bones of the feet.

Make sure that the students learn how to approach the horse before allowing them to vault. Students should understand the run, the takeoff, and the eye contact before vaulting over the horse. It is important that students have proper contact with the takeoff board to avoid running into the horse.

To avoid hurting the lower back, students must be directed not to arch backward on landing. The legs must be flexed at the hips and knees to take up the force.

Initially, all vaults should be practiced at a height that allows for ease of learning. Later, as the mechanics of each skill are fully realized, the horse should be raised.

Make sure that the spotter understands the technique required for each vault. When two spotters are used for the more difficult vaults, make sure that the combination of both spotters is effective.

As with the apparatus already mentioned, the teacher should check the stability of the horse at each position. There should be ample mats for landing, especially when the Mini Tramp is used for practicing certain types of vaults.

When the *pommels* are removed, adhesive tape should be placed over the holes to avoid having a finger slip into them.* If tape is not available, the screws securing the pommels should be replaced after removing each pommel.

*Pommels are the *U*-shaped handles on top of a side horse.

Trampoline

The teacher should always check the trampoline to make sure it is properly set up. Some teachers feel that mats should be placed around the sides of the trampoline for additional protection should the performer fall from the top of the tramp. The trampoline should have pads on the metal frames.

An adequate number of spotters must be positioned around the trampoline. These individuals must realize they are expected to aid the performer should she lose control.

Instructors should teach:

- how to bounce safely
- the proper mechanics for stopping a bounce
- how to execute tuck jumps, straddle jumps, and full turns to enhance the feel for vertical bouncing
- beginner skills such as the sit drop, knee drop, doggy drop; and basic combinations such as a sit drop, doggy drop, forward roll; or, perhaps, a sit drop, straddle into a front drop, stand

If students are allowed to wear gymnastics shoes or socks, they should understand that socks promote uncontrolled bouncing and poor balance. This may, however, be corrected with many hours of practice.

Never allow students to perform with their eyes shut. Moreover, when bouncing on the trampoline, students should be instructed to spot the front of the trampoline to insure better control and balance. Students should be continually challenged to be alert and in control when bouncing on the trampoline. Too often, students become careless and attempt skills beyond their abilities. The teacher should recognize this and intervene when necessary to keep the students on the right track.

Students should not be allowed to try flips without adequate spotting. At first, all flips should be hand spotted until the performer has acquired the essential parts of the skill. Later, with the spotter still on the tramp, the performer should be encouraged to perform the skill. After the student has executed the skill many times with consistency, then the spotter is allowed to move to the end of the tramp to spot. The performer is then asked to perform the flip in the direction of the spotter. Hence, if the performer is asked to perform a front flip, the spotter should be facing the performer.

Students and athletes need to have good fundamentals. Without good basic moves, the execution of more advanced skills becomes increasingly dangerous.

When teaching trampoline skills, do not dwell too long on the explanation. Rather, demonstrate the skill, indicate the main points, then get the students involved. The teacher can go into a full-length discussion of the basic biomechanics at a later time, when the students will be more ready for such a discussion.

When students get off the trampoline, they should be instructed not to jump or bounce toward the side of the tramp. They should walk toward the side of the tramp and then climb down (never jump), and stand close to the tramp like a spotter. Sometimes, it is good to have the students, especially the younger ones, sit on the pad around the *trampoline bed*.* Very small children should be helped on and off the trampoline.

When instructing a student on the trampoline, always stand so that the performer's face can be seen. This is vital, since a teacher must sometimes react to a student's facial expressions. When fear is evident, the teacher should help the student go on to some other less demanding skill.

A special note of concern must be made about closing trampolines. The teacher must be responsible for doing this. If she feels some student help is useful, she should teach them not to have their elbows toward the middle of the tramp when closing it. The elbows should be out to the sides, in the plane of the tramp, to avoid catching an arm should part of the tramp accidentally close too quickly.

Parallel Bars

The bars should always be checked to ensure that they are locked in place. Mats should be placed around and in between the uprights. Be sure other pieces of equipment are moved from the immediate area. The performer should always use enough chalk to keep the hands from slipping off bars. The spotter must be sure the performer has proper arm placement between the bars.

There are numerous beginner skills that can be performed without the teacher or spotters. These include walking across the bars, jumping across the bars, swinging dips, swinging in a straight arm-support position, shoulder stands, single-leg turns, *L* supports, dismounts, and mounts, to mention a few. Beginning students should become aware of these skills. They are especially helpful in developing adequate upper-arm and shoulder strength, which is needed for the more difficult skills. They also aid in the development of a positive attitude toward participating on the bars.

When swinging on the bars or performing a skill requiring a swing, the performer should always

remember to keep the elbows as straight as possible. At first, this will be a conscious process. It helps the performer keep the arms straight if he rotates his elbows laterally, so that the inside of the elbow is more anteriorly positioned.

Students performing on the bars must have some idea of their center of gravity relative to specific skills. For example, the teacher may ask, "Why are your shoulders forward of your hands when your legs are behind your hands?" The reason is of course to keep one's center of gravity as close to the base of support as possible to maintain dynamic balance. This may help the student learn specific skills, since he now has some understanding of why he is asked to perform a certain way.

Although elementary skills seldom require a spotter, one should be used when necessary, particularly for individuals who are not especially strong or coordinated. Also, a spotter may prove psychologically beneficial for reducing the performer's anxiety. Intermediate and advanced skills generally require two spotters. These spotters must know what to expect, the moment of greatest force, and how to control it without injuring either the performer or themselves.

High Bar

As on the parallel bars, the beginner on the high bar must start at a basic level. At no time should a student be allowed to work on giant swings before such moves as a back hip circle, a front hip circle, kips, mill circles, and swinging and turning moves.

The teacher is responsible for the security of the high-bar system. The students are expected to learn the correct progression from one skill to the next. They must also gain an appreciation of the basic biomechanics. By knowing where the greatest force is likely to be during a given skill, both the performer and the spotter will have better control and execution.

When the performer is ready to attempt moves beyond the spotter's control, the teacher must use an overhead spotting belt. An overhead spotting belt is designed to fit around the performer's waist. It consists of ropes running through a series of pulleys attached to the ceiling, usually directly above an apparatus. A single spotter can stand to the side of the performer (e.g., on a trampoline). From here, using the spotting belt, the spotter can help lift the performer into the air or control his descent toward the trampoline when completing a skill.

Like the trampoline, the high bar has a built-in potential for bodily harm, due to the height factor. This is why even the most simple skills require close observation by both spotter and teacher. Nothing can

---

*The *trampoline bed* is the area on which rebound tumbling takes place.

be assumed to be so simple that it will not create problems.

Students must be taught specific grips, such as the forward grip (overgrip), the reverse grip (undergrip), and the mixed grip (over- and undergrip). They should understand that these grips are specific to the direction in which the performer is expected to move. For example, if the student moves forward, using a reverse grip, the hands tend to open and lose contact with the bar. Hence, the use of the hands, as well as hand guards of different types, must be discussed with new students.

Side Horse

For the most part, students and athletes are seldom hurt while performing either basic or advanced skills on this apparatus. The reason for this apparent lack of injuries is that the side horse is fairly close to the floor. If a student misses a move, while still in contact with a pommel, this means dropping only a foot to the floor. This does not mean, however, that someone could not be hurt seriously on the side horse. The point is that it is simply not as dangerous as the parallel bars or the high bar. The force factors are also different with side horse skills when compared, for example, to skills performed on the rings. Injuries that do occur usually result from a failure to lift the legs and hips as high as they should to clear the horse or pommel.

More advanced performers should be aware of the increased force of their required body positions, height, and velocity. It is interesting that even the most difficult side-horse skills can be attempted and practiced without the assistance of a spotter. In this case, the spotter should anticipate certain difficulties in the skill, and be there to break a fall when needed.

Both the teacher and the student are responsible for the proper use and placement of mats, and checking the condition of the side horse.

Rings

When using the rings, always make sure that the mats are positioned under them. The rings should be checked for proper length after being heavily used. Depending on the type of ring set, all aspects of the security system should be checked before class or workout sessions. The rings should be checked for accumulation of chalk and cracking.

Anyone interested in ring work must realize that strength and flexibility are very important. Since the forearm flexors aid in direct control and contact with the rings, the concerned performer must maintain a high degree of forearm strength.

Students must be realistic, and plan to work long, hard hours if they are interested in safely performing such skills as inlocates, dislocates, giant swings, handstands, and crosses. One must first learn the beginner skills; then, with proper training and dedication, more difficult skills will be possible.

Due to the height factor, spotters should always be present when a performer is on the rings. This means that when a student jumps to the rings, pulls to an inverted position, and lowers to a skin-the-cat position, a spotter should stand by the performer to insure the safety of the performer. Very powerful skills should be spotted by two persons. They may decide to spot on top of folded mats, on a bench, or whatever allows the spotter to be as close as possible to the performer. The spotter must always be conscious of the possibility that the performer's hands may come loose from the rings. If this occurs while the performer is moving into or out of a swing, he is likely to end up on his head.

Girls should not be allowed to swing on the rings, just as men should not be allowed to use the women's uneven parallel bars. Simply stated, the majority of the high school and college girls are not strong enough to control their body weight. Thus, their hands are likely to slip with or without the additional force produced by the skills.

Always warm up properly before working the rings. Otherwise, the stress on the shoulders may be too much to maintain proper shoulder stability.

Mini-Tramp

The teacher must first identify problems that may arise if students overlook items such as: (1) the hurdle, (2) the correct use of stored energy as the mat is depressed, and (3) the eye-hand contact necessary to position the body properly on the mat when landing. The spotter must recognize the need to reach in and control the performer should she fail to execute properly the hurdle phase of the approach-landing. The spotter must acknowledge the ever-present possibility that a performer will forget while airborne what she plans to do. Thus, she may approach the Mini Tramp in a very vigorous manner, yet, for example, forget to carry out the basic steps of a front flip.

Although the use of the Mini-Tramp appears to be simple, it can potentially be very dangerous. Since the performer is raising the center of gravity as she performs, the height factor becomes a consideration. The higher the performer is from the mat while performing, the greater the chance of injury should the performance not proceed as expected. Hence, the spotters must be ready to respond quickly to control or modify the performer's actions.

The instructor must learn to present a number of beginner skills that can be used as starters. For example, let us assume that the teacher has taught the jump stretch, the tuck, the straddle, and the full turn. Now, without continuing in difficulty, the teacher can challenge the students by having them perform a forward roll after the execution of each skill. For example, the student may be asked to perform a jump stretch, forward roll combination. It is also a good exercise to have the student perform a forward roll, run, jump stretch, roll combination.

Students in the class should be instructed in various types of spots when advancing from one skill to the next. In this way, students come to appreciate the opportunity to aid the teacher.

When requiring students to combine several skills, the teacher must emphasize the need to think systematically about the skills as they are being performed. Students often concentrate on the second and third skills, and thus fail to execute properly the first. The teacher must emphasize the need to think through the performance before and during its execution.

In just about every aspect of gymnastics, the teacher must help the students believe in themselves so their true potential may be fully realized. The teacher must also help the students to see the need for complete dedication to a specific skill, not just halfway attempts. In the latter case, performers are more prone to injury than when they give it everything possible.

PART 3

SPOTTING TECHNIQUES

6

Acrobatics and Tumbling

Students and gymnasts should learn how to perform basic acrobatic and tumbling skills before they move on to apparatus work. The reason for this is twofold. First, acrobatic and tumbling skills can be learned with less possibility of injury when performed on the mat and later transferred to an apparatus. Second, acrobatic and tumbling skills are recognized as the foundation of gymnastics. Therefore, it is not only safer, but it is the logical place to start gymnastics students. Tumbling skills can also be performed with immediate success, and in a manner that induces the class to keep working together toward a common objective. In this way, even students who are not quite ready to perform on their own will usually do so with a group.

A spotter can help a beginner learn acrobatic and tumbling skills by providing:

- verbal cues and feedback necessary for a safe and less threatening approach to the skills and transitions

- manual assistance necessary to aid the beginner in acquiring the correct "feeling" associated with a given skill or transition

It is the purpose of the chapters in this part to present various spotting techniques used in teaching and coaching students and athletes in gymnastics. The analysis of the spotting technique for a given skill will parallel the illustration. If necessary, the reader must reverse the procedure to accommodate his or her best side. However, use of the so-called best side should probably be reconsidered for at least two reasons:

- When a teacher or student uses only one side to spot from, there is an increased chance of developing what may be referred to as a "strong arm side." Such a person would be unable to spot from both sides with equal force and control.

- If the teacher spots from both sides, this reduces the number of times the spotter must move to adjust for different students.

In essence, the ability to spot with either the right or the left arm increases the effectiveness of the spotter. Sharing the stress of spotting between both arms reduces the wear and tear when one side dominates the other.

The following skills are not presented in the order they must always be taught. Although a reasonable approach has been used in organizing the presentation of the spotting techniques and skills, a teacher may decide to move ahead and attempt skills presented further in the chapter. Should this approach be taken, however, the teacher should feel confident that the students are emotionally and physically ready.

Acrobatic and Tumbling Routines

Although the majority of skills presented in this chapter are performed in the photographs by young female gymnasts, all of them can be performed by male students and athletes. Depending on the types of skills presented, either the teacher or student can develop any number of tumbling routines. They may be designed to permit an easy adaptation to the skills for the new and inexperienced student, or to challenge the more skillful performer. A few of the possibilities are:

1. Forward roll, knee tuck, forward roll
2. Forward roll, straddle jump, forward roll
3. Forward roll, single-leg rise, cartwheel
4. Forward roll, single-leg rise, cartwheel one-half turn, forward roll
5. Forward roll, full turn, forward roll, jump stretch, cartwheel
6. Forward roll, crossover, backward roll extension, backward roll
7. Handstand, forward roll, jump stretch, forward roll, straddle-rise
8. Handstand, forward roll, crossover, backward roll extension
9. Forward roll, single-leg rise, scissor kick, cartwheel
10. Handstand, front limber, forward roll, straddle jump, forward roll
11. Back limber, kick over, backward roll, straddle position, stand
12. Cartwheel, one-half turn, handstand, forward roll, jump stretch

13. Forward roll, single-leg rise, one-arm cartwheel
14. Backward roll, crossover, forward roll, jump stretch, dive roll
15. Frog stand, headstand, forward roll, straddle-rise, forward roll
16. Shoulder roll, cartwheel, handstand, forward roll, stand
17. Run, *tour jeté*, cartwheel, cartwheel, one-half turn, handstand
18. Forward roll, single-leg rise, front limber, headspring, stand
19. Forward roll, single-leg rise, front walkover, handstand, roll-out
20. Forward roll, single-leg rise, run, front handspring step-out
21. Front walkover, cartwheel, back walkover
22. Front walkover, scissors kick, one-arm cartwheel, back walkover
23. Front walkover, cartwheel, back walkover, back roll extension
24. Back roll extension, straddle-down, back roll, stand
25. Back roll extension, back handspring, back roll, stand
26. Back handspring, back roll extension, back roll, stand
27. Run, front handspring step-out, cartwheel, one-half turn, roll-out
28. Run, front handspring step-out, front handspring, stand
29. Run, front handspring, forward roll, headspring
30. Run, front handspring, front flip, forward roll
31. Run, front flip step-out, cartwheel, handstand, forward roll
32. Run, front flip step-out, round-off, back flip
33. Run, front handspring, front flip, front handspring, front flip
34. Run, front handspring, front flip, forward roll, headspring
35. Back walkover, backward roll extension, back handspring
36. Back walkover, handstand, back handspring, jump stretch, back roll
37. Run, side aerial, round-off, jump stretch, back roll extension
38. Run, round-off, back handspring, back flip
39. Run, round-off, back handspring, back handspring, back flip
40. Run, round-off, back dive one-half turn, forward roll, jump stretch
41. Run, front handspring, pike front flip, front headspring
42. Run, round-off, back handspring, full twisting back flip
43. Run, round-off, back handspring, double full twist back flip
44. Run, round-off, back handspring, double back flip
45. Run, front aerial, run, round-off, full twist back flip

Handstand

The handstand position requires that the performer:

1. spread the fingers to increase the area of the base

2. position the hands under the shoulders to attain the desired stretched out appearance

3. maintain straight arms via extended elbow joints

4. extend in (or raise) the shoulders to aid in avoiding an arched position

5. keep the head slightly up to see the hands

6. contract the abdomen muscles to control the lumbar curve; this results in a straighter handstand *

7. position the hips above the shoulders, with the legs straight and feet pointed

*The *lumbar curve* is the curve or arch in the lower back.

Yoga Handstand

This handstand is indeed unique, especially when contrasted to the more common fully extended handstand position. Although the yoga handstand is usually not held for any length of time, women gymnasts pass through such a position as an outcome of various sequences of floor exercise. The spotter can assist the performer by placing pressure on the lower back and abdomen while the desired position is attained. The performer should be able to see her legs and maintain balance at the same time.

1

2

3

1

2

3

1

2

3

Frog Stand to Headstand

1. The teacher has the students place their knees against their elbows. The hands are positioned about shoulder width apart to establish a reasonably large base. This aids control for movement of the performer's center of gravity and helps prevent loss of balance.

2. The performer keeps his head up and balances his body over the hands, moving into the frog stand position. Note that the knees are positioned on the elbows, with the feet pointed.

3. The base is enlarged as the head moves toward the mat, becoming the third contact point. The larger the base, the easier it is to maintain balance. The performer should be encouraged to keep most of his weight on the arms.

4. The headstand position is achieved by gradually raising the hips to a point above the shoulders. The performer's body weight should still be mostly on the arms. Thus the hips should remain positioned between the head and the hands, not directly over the head. The legs should be straight, and the feet pointed.

Although a spotter is not illustrated in this sequence, there is sometimes a need to use one or more to avoid excessive pressure around the neck area.

Straight-Straight Press to Straddle Handstand

1. The performer must flex at the hips and place his hands in between and forward of the feet. The head should be high enough to allow for visual contact of the base, the hands.

2. By means of a gradual to more acute forward lean of the shoulders, the hips are raised above the base. The upward motion of the hips is a result of intense muscle contraction of the trunk and hip flexors. The feet are kept pointed.

3. As the hips move above the hands, the legs are raised (via hip extension) to the straddle position noted in the illustration (step 3). At this point, the performer usually closes the legs to perform the handstand as it is normally done. However, in this instance the legs remain in the straddled position to highlight a major principle of balance. That is, when the legs are kept apart, the center of gravity is closer to the base. This makes balancing a little easier, especially for the beginning student. Balance is also easier when the arms are slightly flexed at the elbows, as this lowers the center of gravity. A spotter should be encouraged to stand to the side of the performer to aid during the upward motion of the hips. The performer should be instructed not to jump, but instead to assume gradually the desired hip flexion and position noted in step 2.

Frog Stand to Planche

1-2. The reader should refer to the first skill (Frog Stand to Headstand) for clarification of steps 1 and 2.

3. The planche is generally recognized as a fairly difficult skill. It is obviously a strength move, and yet with a good sense of balance it becomes a balance move, too. The performer must be able to withstand pressure about the wrist and fingers during the forward lean of the shoulders to allow for necessary movement of the center of gravity toward the base. Remember, this move is possible because the performer is capable of leaning forward just to the point where the center of gravity is over the hands. This process is easier with the legs straddled than when they are kept together. When they are kept together, the forward lean of the shoulders must be exaggerated to allow for greater movement of the performer's center of gravity.

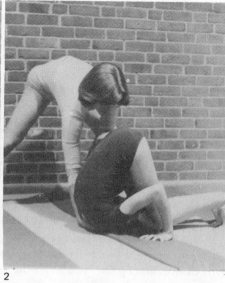
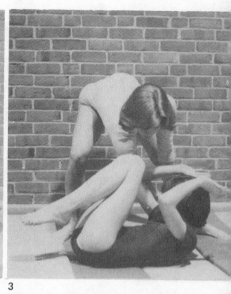

1

2

3

1

2

3

4

5

1

2

3

4

Forward Roll

1. The spotter should place her outside hand at the performer's neck to assist her in moving the head toward the chest. Note the lean to the spotter's left, and the position of the spotter's feet. Thus the spotter starts in front of the student, not at her side.

2. As the student places her head on the mat, the spotter should maintain contact with her neck to insure correct body position. When necessary, the spotter should also provide a push with her left arm at the performer's thigh.

3. As the student nears completion of the skill, the spotter should continue to assist by providing pressure at the neck. The major part of the skill, properly tucking the chin and performing the roll safely, is completed by this point.

4. The spotter provides additional support at the student's back to aid her in reaching a standing position.

7

Forward Roll, Full Turn, Forward Roll

1. By this point, the student should have already learned how to perform the forward roll unassisted. Now the spotter is in position to spot the skill.

2. The student begins by tucking the chin to commence the forward roll. A controlled push with the legs provides sufficient force to displace the center of gravity forward of the base. The forward-downward motion of the body is controlled by the muscles at the posterior aspect of the student's arms. These muscles, the triceps brachii, contract eccentrically as the elbows flex.*

3-4. As the student moves from the tuck position to execute the full turn, the spotter assumes a more active role in anticipation of poor mechanics. In this case, when the performer is just about to contact the mat (step 4), the spotter should touch the hips to aid in maintaining balance. Note how the spotter flexes at the knees when contacting the performer. This allows for better stability, and thus better control of the performer should it become necessary to alter a poor attempt.

5-7. These three shots demonstrate the recovery and forward roll to finish.

* *Eccentric* muscular contraction means that the muscle contracts while it is lengthening. In other words, the triceps contract as the elbow is flexed.

Forward Roll, Straddle Jump

1-2. The spotting procedures for the forward roll have been explained in the instructions for the forward roll.

3-4. As the performer completes the roll and begins her jump stretch into the straddle position, the spotter stands to the side and waits for the right moment to contact the waist. The spotter must allow the performer plenty of room during the upward motion of the legs. To do this quickly and carefully, the spotter should assume a position slightly in back of the performer during the upward thrust of the legs. In this way, he can reach in and contact the performer as noted in photos 3 and 4. After the performer touches the feet with her hands, the legs will return very quickly to the mat for support and continuation of the sequence. The spotter can assist in controlling the force on contacting the mat, as well as providing some additional force for execution of subsequent skills.

1

2

3

1

2

3

2

1

3

4

Forward Roll, Single-Leg Rise

1. As the performer begins the forward roll, the spotter positions his hand at the neck to assist with the tucking action. The spotter is positioned slightly in front of the performer's hands, where the action will be realized. Note that the spotter's legs are flexed at both the hips and knees, allowing for more control of the performer.

2. The spotter contacts the performer at the waist to aid her in extending the right knee. To do this properly, the spotter must allow the performer to move in front of him.

3. As the performer extends the right knee and points the foot, she gradually assumes a more upright position. The spotter aids her by flexing at the elbows, dropping his center of gravity, and increasing his base.

Backward Roll

1. Although any number of different body positions can be used to enter safely into the backward roll, the position depicted in photo 1 is the most common one used. The spotter positions herself in back of the student, and establishes hand contact. Contact is necessary at this point because some students drop the back toward the floor instead of sitting into the roll. Sitting can be encouraged by placing a hand at the hip area to create sufficient hip flexion to cause the performer to sit into the skill. Note the wide base of the spotter, as well as her distance behind the performer.

2. As the performer rolls into the skill and the hands touch the mat, the spotter can assist by contacting the hips and providing both an upward and backward motion sufficient to relieve pressure about the performer's neck and shoulder region. The spotter should not push the performer over, since improper position of the head may injure the neck. It is necessary, especially when the performer demonstrates a lack of upper arm strength, to lift and position the performer's hips above the hands.

3. Notice that the spotter moves from a flexed left knee and hip to a fully extended left leg in step 3. This type of transition represents the dynamic aspect necessary for excellent spotting. The spotter moves with the performer to aid her when a deficiency is evident.

Two-Arm Cartwheel ✳

1. In photo 1, note the beginning stances of both spotter and performer. As the performer begins the cartwheel, the arms should be raised above the shoulders. The performer places one leg in front of the other. The performer's beginning stance alerts the spotter which side she must stand on. For example, with the performer's right leg forward, her right hand will contact the mat first, with the left hand following. It is important that the spotter stand on the correct side, since spotters usually spot the beginning students from the performer's backside, as in the photos. When the performer can execute the cartwheel reasonably well, the exercise can be safely spotted from either side.

2. As the performer flexes at the hip, and leans forward to place the right hand on the mat, the spotter makes contact first with her left hand and then with her right. Both contacts should be at performer's waist. Note the spotter's wide base and the forward position of the performer.

3. The spotter maintains contact at the waist to aid the performer in keeping the arms straight. The performer's head should be raised so she can see the mat. The hands should contact the mat one at a time; this is also true of the feet in step 4. Note that the spotter is leaning forward on her right leg to assist the performer in continuing through the skill. If the performer's legs are not kept straight and wide apart, the spotter should inform her so she can make the desired corrections.

4. As the performer's left foot contacts the mat, it is usually necessary to provide some help at the waist to keep the body moving over the newly formed base. Hence, a small push with the right hand, in this case, aids performer in raising the shoulders and assuming a position similar to that in step 1.

1   2   3   4

1   2   3

1   2   3   4   5

Two-Arm Cartwheel Turn into Side Split

1. In step 1, the spotter should closely observe the performer. The spotter must be ready to spot, and to react to the forward motion of the performer.

2. As the performer moves into the handstand part of the cartwheel, the spotter should contact both hips to stabilize her. The spotter's left hand contacts the performer to help her attain the inverted position.

3-4. As the performer begins the quick reversing action necessary to bring the left leg into the side split, the spotter's right hand supports the performer's weight and controls the de-

scent. Hence, the spotter helps the performer lower herself to the mat. Note the spotter's wide base. The more stable the spotter, the more effective the spotting technique.

5. The spotter's right hand remains in contact with the performer while the left releases. This provides the room for the performer to straighten her back.

One-Arm Cartwheel

1-2. The one-arm cartwheel is spotted just like the two-arm cartwheel. As the performer leans into the skill, the spotter reaches in and contacts the waist, first on the hip-flexed side then on the other. Hence, the initial contact is the spotter's left hand on the performer's right hip. The second contact point is the spotter's right hand on the performer's left hip. Since the performer is using only one arm to support the body, the spotter may have to exert himself a bit harder to insure a safe performance. The performer should be instructed to circle the non-support arm to aid in the upward and

forward motion of the hips.

3-4. As the performer's left leg contacts the mat, the spotter usually provides additional support to help the performer avoid pressure around the ankle and knee. All beginners should be taught the cartwheel using the "front" rather than the "side" approach. That is, the performer should be encouraged to begin the cartwheel with the abdomen facing the direction in which the skill is to be performed. On completion of the skill, the abdomen should be facing the direction in which the skill was performed. The photos for this skill demonstrate this approach.

Handstand Front Limber *

1. As the performer positions herself to begin the first skill, the spotter should make the appropriate adjustments. The spotter's left hand is positioned at the performer's right hip to assist in moving the hips up above the hands. The spotter also reaches across the performer's back to contact the left thigh and aid in positioning it above the hips.

2. Note that the spotter's stance is wide, with a low center of gravity for increased stability. Although the illustration depicts the spotter on the hip-flexed side of the performer, the spotter can also spot from the swing-

leg side just as effectively by (1) placing one hand across the back to contact the hip area; and (2) grasping the swing leg with the arm closest to it. In essence, this approach is the reverse of steps 1 and 2.

3. Once the performer assumes the handstand position, the spotter moves her hands to the thighs or knees. At this time, it is helpful to offer some verbal encouragement to the performer to help the performer achieve the desired body position.

4. As the performer moves from step 3 to 4, the spotter quickly removes her hands from the legs so as not to disturb the forward motion. The spotter's

right hand contacts the lower back to provide support as the performer realizes the bridge-up position.

5. The spotter then places her left hand at the performer's shoulder or arm to aid in the upward motion of the upper trunk. The right hand continues to provide assistance until the performer's center of gravity is again over the base, the feet.

1   2   3

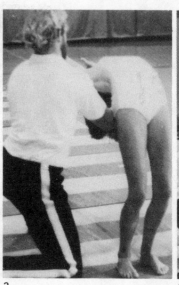

1   2   3   4

1   2   3   4   5

Front Walkover

1. Although the spotter's left hand is positioned in front of the performer, it quickly moves to the lower back area as the front walkover begins. Note the forward position of the spotter relative to the performer.

2. As the performer places her hands on the mat and begins to pass through the handstand position, the spotter assumes more responsibility for the safety of the performer by: (a) supporting the lower back with the left hand and arm; and (b) grasping the right thigh to help keep the leg elevated throughout the skill.

3. Notice that the movement of the spotter was first toward the left (see step 1) and then the right. The spotter's upper body is basically vertical, and the legs flex at the knees and hips to keep from interfering with the walkover. The spotter should be aware of the performer's ability to rise out of the arched position. If the performer cannot pull out without undue strain to the rest of the body, it may be more helpful and safer to use an alternate spotting technique. In this instance, the spotter should instead place her left hand about the performer's right arm and her right hand at the performer's lower back. These contacts will help the performer by reducing the stress in the abdomen and hip musculature.

Headspring

1. The spotter should instruct the performer to place her hands and head in basically the same position as if she were executing a headstand. The only difference is that the head and neck should be slightly more extended to encourage the arch in step 3. The legs must remain straight, or else the arms must work extremely hard via elbow extension to raise the hips to a height sufficient to land safely.

2. The role of the spotter is to aid the performer in getting into the desired body position. For example, he must encourage her to lean forward with the hips while keeping the legs straight.

Just as she is about to lose her balance, she should very quickly extend the hips and then push vigorously with the arms. The spotter aids extension of the elbows with his left arm.

3. To lessen impact on landing, the spotter continues to lift the performer at the lower back using the right hand. The left arm aids the performer in straightening the body.

4. Note the hand placements of the spotter. Also, observe that the spotter's right hip and knee move from flexion to a more extended position as the performer moves through steps 1 to 4.

Back Handspring

1. It is important for the spotter to have her hands on the performer before beginning the backward motion. When spotting from the performer's left side, the spotter should place her right hand across the lower back to the right hip to properly control the sitting and circular motions. The left hand is at the left thigh to provide an upward force should the performer fail to provide enough herself.

2. As the performer sits into the back handspring, the spotter's right hand becomes a critical factor in maintaining the correct body thrust. If too much pressure is applied at the back, the performer will move vertically and hence not acquire the desired mechanics. The performer must understand the role that her arms play in attaining the correct backward thrust. The arms should be positioned close to the head, as the neck is extended in an effort to see the mat.

3-4. Once pressure is realized about the arms and shoulders, the spotter should aid the performer by helping provide the circular motion necessary to get the legs back on the mat. This is done with the left arm.

5. As the beginning student completes the backward thrust, the spotter should maintain contact with the lower back to prevent an uncontrolled backward spin.

1   2

1   2   3   4

1   2   3   4

Back Limber

1. The starting position for the performer is depicted in the illustration. The spotter places her right hand at the performer's lower back and the left hand at the posterior-lateral aspect of the thigh. Note the spotter's wide base, as well as the forward lean on the left leg in the direction of the performer.

2. As the performer arches backward to touch the mat, the spotter controls the motion until the hands contact the mat. The performer's arms should be straight, and the feet should maintain contact with the mat. The spotter should encourage the performer to keep her head back and up so that she can see the mat. The legs should be kept as straight as possible to aid in lifting the abdomen. The arms should be as near vertical as possible.

Back Walkover

1. As the performer assumes the correct body position to begin the back walkover, the spotter places her right hand at the lower back area and the left hand behind the knee or thigh of the forward leg.

2. As the performer's arms move backward to contact the mat, the spotter supports the back with the right hand and arm. The spotter assists the swing leg with the left hand. The spotter's base should be very wide, with the body basically vertical. That is, while the knees and hips are flexed, the upper trunk is only slightly forward. The spotter must remain erect as possible to keep from being hit by the performer. This is accomplished via a wide base and properly positioned shoulders and arms.

3. The performer's hips move to a position above the hands, with the legs spread in a split. The right hand of the spotter continues to assist in proper movement and control of the hips, while the left hand provides the impetus to maintain the circular motion of the legs. At this point, the right hand of the spotter is very critical in the continuation of the skill.

4. The spotter places her right hand at the lower back of the performer to complete the back walkover. Note that the performer finishes with her hands positioned above the shoulders. Her body weight, initially supported by her left leg, is now supported primarily by her right leg. Therefore, to begin another back walkover (assuming the same sequence) it would be necessary to rock backward until the left leg again assumes full support as in step 1.

Back Walkover into Split

1. Since the performer is supporting herself on the left leg, the spotter realizes she will be lifting the right leg as the swing leg. Therefore, he positions himself so that the right hand supports the lower back and the left hand contacts the right leg.

2. The spotter's right hand aids in the upward rotation of the hips, while the left hand helps maintain the desired leg position. The support at the back is the more important of the two hand contacts.

3-4. As the performer's hips move past vertical, the spotter's right hand quickly moves from the back to the abdomen to support the body on the descent phase of the skill. The spotter's left arm now contacts the performer's left arm and shoulder to help control the forward motion of the shoulders during this final phase.

1   2   3   4

1   2   3

1   2   3

Round-Off Back Handspring

1-2. The spotter must position himself on the mat where the round-off will be completed. Notice that the spotter is very active during step 1. As the performer's legs contact the mat and she quickly moves into the back handspring, the spotter assumes a position whereby he can control the backward thrust with the right hand (step 2). The performer's arms should remain straight throughout the sequence.

3-4. The spotter continues to maintain contact with the performer to insure that she does not overspin the skill. His right hand is placed at the back to assist the performer in acquiring the correct body recovery following the sequence.

Side Aerial (Spotting Both Hips)

1. As the performer positions herself with the right foot forward to provide the necessary upward lift, the spotter quickly places his left hand at her right hip. The performers left leg is used to develop motion upward and forward to realize the body position in step 2. Note that the spotter starts out in front of the performer, and not to her side, as the skill begins.

2. The spotter secures the performer's left hip with his right hand. Now, with both hips held tightly by the spotter, the performer is suspended above the mat via flexion at the elbows and extension at the shoulder joints.

3-4. As the performer places her swing leg on the mat, the spotter gradually releases the tension at the hips. Students should not be encouraged to learn this skill unless they have mastered the one- and two-arm cartwheels and have an efficient spotter present.

Side Aerial (Spotting One Hip)

1. The spotter should tell the performer where he would like her to begin the skill. Note that the spotter is on the mat when the skill begins. If the spotter attempts to move from the floor to the mat, he risks catching his foot on the edge of the mat.

2. The spotter must be sensitive to the amount of pressure on the performer at the hip area. Too much pressure is more dangerous than too little, since an overspin may result in an uncontrolled series of recovery moves. Note that the spotter has both legs flexed at the knees, as well as the hips, in an effort to get "under the action." Both the upward thrust of the arms and extension of the knees and hips are necessary to position the performer properly. If the skill is progressing as it should, the spotter may decide to remove his arms from the performer's hips and allow her to land without assistance. If he feels that the performer is likely to overspin, then he should make an effort to contact the outside hip.

3. The spotter very quickly moves his hands from the performer's right to her left hip to assist the landing. It is not always necessary to use both hands as noted in step 3. In fact, most spotters would probably contact the performer's left hip with the right hand while removing the left hand from the performer altogether.

1　　2　　3

1　　2　　3　　4

1　　2　　3　　4　　5

Front Aerial

1. As the performer places her right foot close to the spotter to begin the front aerial, the spotter contacts the abdomen to assist with the upward phase of the skill.

2. The spotter's right hand moves to the performer's back to help position the body correctly. Note that the spotter gradually needs to get below the performer. Although this is not always necessary, it is indicative of the spotter's intent to do an excellent job of assisting the performer.

3. The spotter's right hand reduces the force upon landing, as well as aiding in the followthrough of the skill. The spotter may vary this technique, using only his left hand (if the recovery is safe) or his right hand (if the takeoff is reasonably high).

Back Flip

1. The spotter should always encourage the performer to begin the back flip by raising the arms above the shoulders. Note that the spotter contacts the performer's lower back and stands behind her.

2. The performer quickly flexes at the hips and legs to generate the necessary muscle power to elevate the body vertically. The spotter assists the performer by aiding her during the upward-backward thrust.

3-4. As the performer stretches upward and backward with the legs flexing tightly at the knees and hips, the spotter continues to support the lower back with the right hand. The spotter's left hand contacts the thigh to create the desired angular rotation.

5. As the landing is realized, the spotter should maintain contact with the lower back to prevent excessive force on the knee joints or to prevent the performer from possibly overspinning.

Back Dive One-Half Turn to Handstand Round-Off

1. The spotter and performer should understand that this skill is a lead-up to the full twisting back flip illustrated two skills later. To begin with, the spotter contacts the lower back both to let the performer know he is ready and to aid during upward thrust of the arms and body.

2-3. The performer's arms are raised above the shoulders as she turns in the direction of the spotter. Both of the spotter's arms are outstretched to position the performer properly.

4-5. The spotter flexes on the right side to allow for movement of the performer's body toward the floor. Note that the spotter's left arm is still horizontally positioned to aid in movement through the handstand.

6. The performer should quickly execute the one-half turn to complete the sequence.

1   2   3   4

1   2   3   4

1   2   3   4

Full Twisting Back Flip

1. The spotter places his left hand at the performer's lower back to assist during the back and upward phase.

2. The spotter's left arm is horizontally positioned as the performer begins the initial phase of the full twist. Remember, the full twisting back flip is a combination of two moves: (a) a back dive with a one-half twist, and (b) a round-off without hands (i.e., a *barani*). Note that the spotter stands on the side where the performer started her twist.

3-4. As the performer nears the vertical position, the spotter provides additional control by grasping both hips. Note that the spotter's elbows are flexed in photos 3 and 4 to help the performer maintain the desired height. By flexing at the hips, the performer begins the downward movement of the legs toward the mat.

5. The performer's hips and knees are flexed to reduce the force of landing. The spotter should maintain contact until the performer is under control.

Front Flip

1. For this skill, two spotters provide better control of the performer. Note that the spotters contact the performer at the abdomen, using the hand nearest her.

2. As the performer becomes airborne, the spotters contact the performer's back with their outside arms to assist with the rotational aspect of the skill.

3-4. Note that both spotters have their arms crossed as the performer lands. The first hand of each spotter to contact the performer provides the necessary upward lift, as well as preventing the performer from overspinning. The spotters' opposite hands are primarily responsible for supporting the performer during the descent phase. Note the spotters' hands on the lower back in photo 2.

Several other spotting techniques are worth mentioning at this time. For example, when a student can just about perform the front flip, it is sometimes helpful to contact the abdomen with just the nearest hand. When more force is needed, both hands can be used at the same time to enhance the vertical thrust of the skill. This approach is similar to the technique used for spotting the side aerial, using one hip. Like the side aerial, it is also necessary to anticipate an overspin and be ready to reach in and contact the performer.

Front Handspring, Front Flip

1. The spotter stands approximately where the performer will finish the front handspring.

2. Just as the handspring is completed, the spotter places his left hand on the performer's abdomen. The spotter must be very quick to accomplish this.

3-4. As the performer advances into the second skill, the spotter's left hand aids in the upward thrust, and his right hand aids the rotational part of the front flip. These two hand contacts must be made quickly and without hesitation if the performer is not to be missed.

5. If the front flip is spotted correctly, the spotter's arms will be crossed as the performer lands. Note that the first hand contact provides the necessary lift, as well as control for excessive spin. An interesting variation for spotting this sequence involves two spotters, in which one spots the front handspring (providing extra lift) and the second spots the front flip.

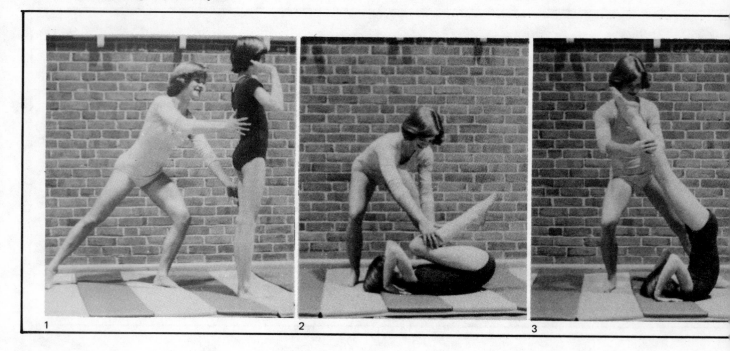

1   2   3

Back Roll Extension to Handstand

1. To insure sufficient force upon extension of the legs, the performer begins from the standing position. The longer the distance through which the center of gravity is moved, the greater the force realized at step 3. Note that the spotter has hand contact at step 1. This is necessary to prevent the performer from arching backward to the floor.

2-3. As the performer nears completion of the back roll, the hips and legs are vigorously elevated to a position above the hands. The spotter must very quickly reach in and contact the knees or thighs to provide guidance in the direction of the desired leg and hip thrust. If the performer lacks sufficient upper arm and shoulder strength to reach step 4, the spotter must supply the extra strength. When this is necessary, the spotter should flex at the knees and hips as in steps 2 and 3, and then quickly straighten the joints to assume the position in step 4.

4. The spotter should help guide the performer to the desired body position. She should also inform the performer of any errors, such as poor shoulder position, head held too high, arch in the lower back, legs apart and flexed at the knees, and failure to point toes.

Shoulder Balance

1. The spotter positions herself along the beam so that her right hand is at the performer's left hip and her left hand is on the right hip. The performer should begin the movement of the hands along the beam toward her neck.

2. As the performer raises her legs above the shoulders, she should be instructed to grasp the beam very tightly to reduce any chance of falling. The spotter helps by holding the hips, thus keeping the body in line with the beam.

Side Split to V Seat

1. As the performer assumes the side split position, the spotter assists by placing her left hand at the performer's lower back and the other just above the right ankle. Both contacts will help the performer maintain an upright position over the beam. While there are a variety of ways to acquire this position, the beginner should first be encouraged to assume a squat position on the beam. Then she should extend the legs slowly until she attains a full side split.

2. From the side split position, the performer brings the left leg forward to assume the V seat, as in photo 2.

The spotter helps by positioning her left hand on the performer's back, while the other hand contacts both legs. The left hand, being the more important of the two, should keep the performer from falling backward. Naturally, both skills must be learned on the floor and the low beam before they are attempted on the high beam.

Tuck-Vault, Mount Squat Turn

1. The performer mounts the beam in a tucked position. The spotter usually stands in front of the beam, and helps by supporting the hips and stabilizing the arms.

2-3. Turning to the left, the performer assumes a squat position, with the left foot in front of the right.

4-5. By extending the knees and hips, the performer's center of gravity is raised. It is raised even higher as she plantar flexes the feet. The higher the center of gravity from the beam—the base—the more susceptible she becomes to minor faults. At this time, the spotter should encourage the performer to concentrate on the beam in front of her.

6. As the performer flexes at the knees, she returns to a squat position with her left foot in front of the right. The arms are positioned to complement the body expression.

1   2   3   4

1   2   3   4

1   2   3   4

Stride Leap

1-2. The performer's body weight is supported by the right foot. The left foot is the swing leg, allowing another step prior to the leap. Note that the spotter is holding the performer's left hand.

3. As the performer pushes off with the left foot, the right foot is quickly elevated to a horizontal position. Both legs are spread, giving the impression of a wide stride leap. Even while the student is in the air, the spotter should maintain hand contact.

4-5. It is important for the spotter to realize that if the right foot of the performer fails to land squarely on the beam, she could be seriously hurt. Hence, there is always the need to be very cautious. Note that the spotter has her eyes on the performer. The performer must also be serious about the fundamentals of the skill. The force from the leap is dissipated by knee flexion, controlled by *eccentric* muscle contraction of the quadriceps.* That is, the muscles on the anterior aspect of the thigh contract while they are lengthening to ensure that knee flexion is in accord with the desired body position.

---

* *Eccentric* muscle contraction refers to contraction of a muscle or muscle group while it lengthens.

Full Turn on One Leg to Lunge

1. The performer is in the stance necessary to begin the full turn. Her left arm is raised to a forward position. It will move horizontally backward to provide part of the force to carry the body around on the left foot. The right arm will provide some force as well. Finally, the push of the right foot against the beam will help, due to Newton's Third Law of Motion (action-reaction).

2-3. As the right leg is flexed at the knee and hip, coupled with the forces previously mentioned, the performer will begin to spin about the longitudinal axis (i.e., from the head to the feet). Note that the left foot is plantar flexed, thus raising the center of gravity. This makes the balancing process more difficult.

4. As the spin nears completion, the performer extends the right leg to make contact with the beam, as noted in the illustration. At this point, the enlarged base and the flexed right knee allow for easy balance, since the center of gravity becomes closer to the beam. Naturally, the position of the arms also helps in maintaining balance.

Headstand

1-2. From the starting position, the performer flexes at the hips and places her hands on the top part of the beam. The legs remain straight while the arms flex at the elbows. As the performer moves closer to the beam, the spotter should reach forward and establish contact.

3-4. As the head is placed on the beam, the spotter should secure the waist and encourage the performer to raise the legs to the position noted in photo 4. The performer should raise the legs to a vertical position. While this is being realized, the spotter should maintain a tight grip at both sides of the performer. More specifically, the spotter's right hand grasps the performer's left side, while her left hand contacts the performer's right side. The spotter must provide sufficient control to keep the performer from placing too much pressure on the neck area.

1 2 3 4

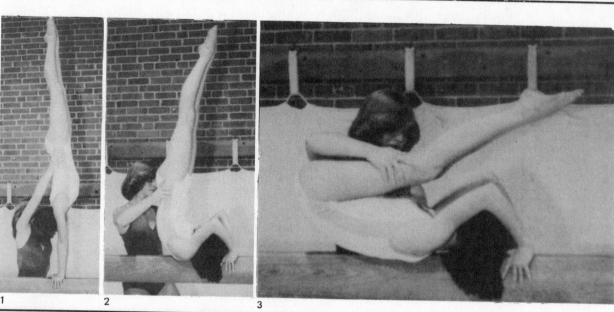

1 2 3

1

2

3

Handstand to Headstand (Straddle-Leg Position)

1-2. Note the forward position of the spotter, as well as her wide stance for better control of the performer. As the performer's hands are placed on the beam, the spotter reaches in and secures the performer's hips, as in step 2.

3. As the performer flexes the elbows, placing the head on the beam, the spotter moves backward, maintaining control of the hips. Note that the spotter is spotting behind, rather than to the side of the performer.

4-5. While the spotter maintains contact with the hips, the performer spreads the legs to a straddle split. From here, the performer could go into one of many different skills. In the forward roll, for instance, the legs would come together. In this regard, the spotter is properly positioned to assist the performer.

Handstand Forward Roll

1. Step 1 illustrates the front spotting technique described earlier.

2. The performer flexes the elbows to allow for lowering of the body and subsequent movement into the mechanics of the roll. The spotter continues to keep a firm grip about the hips to insure that the performer's neck and back are not injured on contact with the beam. Note that the spotter moves ahead of the performer in the direction in which she will move. Also, note that the spotter's feet are wide apart to improve balance so she can control the performer.

3. Once the performer is on her back, she should reach under the beam to reduce any unnecessary movement. The spotter should move slightly to the side of the performer's hips.

Handstand

1. The spotter verbally encourages the performer to assume the correct body position and to give an all-out effort. The spotter waits for performer with raised hands in anticipation of contacting the hips.

2. As the performer's hands contact the beam, she should push with the right leg and swing the left up and over the base. Assistance is provided with the arms and hands, as illustrated in step 2. Note that the spotter's left side is in direct contact with the beam. This is important, since it enlarges the spotter's base, improving stability and efficiency.

3. Note that the spotter is facing the performer, rather than standing to her side. This particular position is the best one for effective control of the performer's forward motion, should the upward motion of the legs be too great. The forward position of the spotter also provides excellent control of the performer if she should quickly flex the arms and neck when moving into a forward roll from the handstand position. Lastly, by not standing directly to the performer's side, there will be more room for the performer to push to the side if there is a need to dismount.

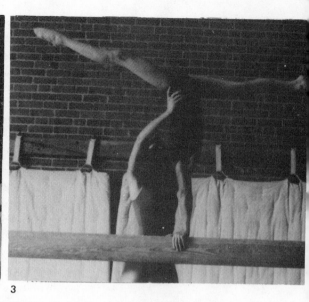

1   2   3

1   2   3   4   5

1   2   3

Handstand (Split Position)

1. As the performer places her hands on the beam, the spotter moves to make contact with the hips. The spotter's right hand goes to the performer's left side while the left hand contacts the right. As the swing leg is kicked upward, the spotter will have to tighten her grip to maintain control.

2. The spotter should maintain contact with the performer both physically and verbally. If the performer starts to lose control, the spotter should tell her to push to one side of the beam and dismount.

3. The spotter should place her abdomen against the beam to stabilize herself. Note that the spotter's hand contacts remain the same while the legs are spread.

Handstand (Split Position) to Side Split

1-2. As the performer places her hands on the beam, the spotter should quickly contact the lower back with the right hand. The push leg of the performer is gripped with the left hand. The spotter's right hand helps the performer by lessening the downward pressure of her body on the arms.

3-4. While maintaining contact with the lower back, the spotter moves with the performer's right leg to assist in placing the leg on the beam. Note that the performer must raise her left arm to allow the right leg to come to a rest position on the beam. Since this is not an easy move to perform, there is a need for excellent spotting.

5. The spotter's arms are crossed, with the right hand on the performer's left hip and the left hand on the right hip, respectively. It is important to keep contact, since the performer may need a few moments to feel relaxed.

Handstand, Front Limber

1. As the performer leans forward to place the hands on the beam, the spotter reaches up to contact the right hip with his left hand. Note that the spotter is in front of the performer. Also, observe that the spotter's right hand is elevated in anticipation of contacting the performer's left hip, as in step 2.

2. To secure the handstand position, the spotter maintains control at both hips. When necessary, the spotter should verbally encourage responses that will result in a better and safer performance.

3. As the performer moves her legs forward of the base, the spotter quickly moves his left hand from the performer's right hip to her lower back. This contact point helps control the influence of gravity on the forward and downward motion of the legs and body. The spotter's right hand moves quickly from the performer's left hip to the legs to aid in placement of the feet on the beam. These arm movements should be started the moment the performer begins the front limber.

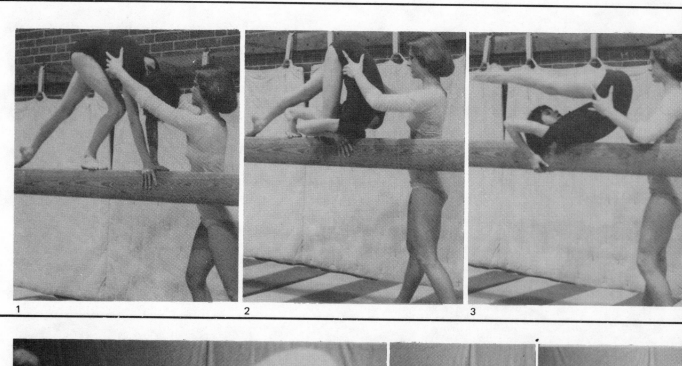

1   2   3

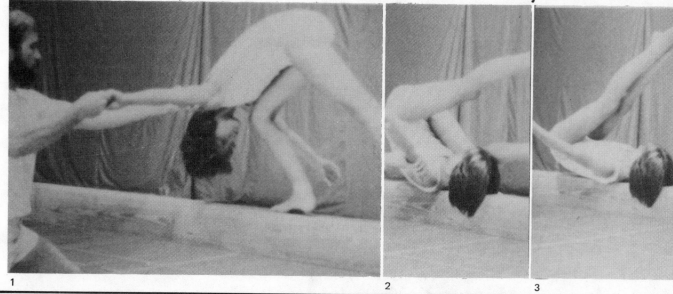

1   2   3

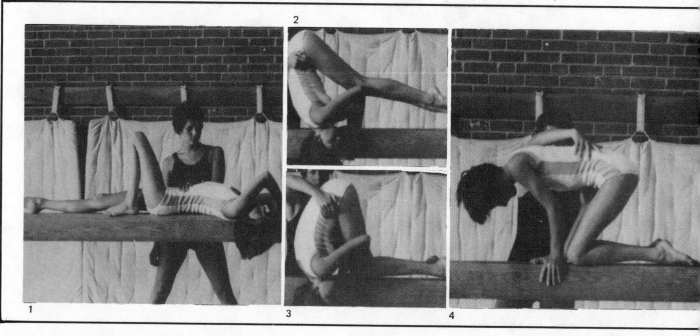

1   2   3   4

Forward Roll

1. As the performer places her hands on the beam and positions her body for the skill, the spotter stands in front and reaches upward to contact and control the performer. Generally, the spotter must encourage the beginning student to raise the hips prior to tucking the head.

2. When the performer's head is placed between the hands, the legs should gradually be brought together. The spotter should guide the performer along the beam, contacting the performer as noted in the illustration. At this point, the spotter should be sure the performer reaches under the beam to aid in control of the roll.

3. By this stage the performer has completed the forward roll and is now in the process of controlling her position on the beam. This is done by: (a) maintaining a tight grip under the beam, and (b) keeping the legs straight and directly above the beam. Although not illustrated, the spotter usually moves to the performer's side at this point to allow forward progression of the legs.

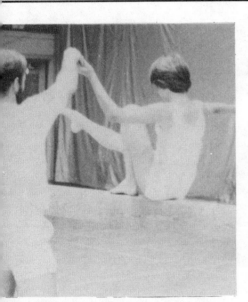

Forward Roll (No Hands)

1. As the performer assumes the correct body position to commence the roll without hands, the spotter aids by maintaining contact with the left arm. The spotter stands in front of the performer and alongside the beam.

2. This part of the skill is probably the most difficult, since poorly directed forward movement could cause the performer to roll off the beam. The spotter must help by controlling the direction of the roll using his left arm. Note that he has contact at both the hand and the arm. Also, note that the spotter is observing the skill intently.

3. This aspect of the skill is relatively easy, since the performer is already moving smoothly through the skill. The spotter simply observes the performer's movements at this point.

4. As the performer attempts the single-leg maneuver, however, upward motion of the spotter's arm may be necessary to aid the performer's left leg during the extension process.

Back Shoulder Roll to Knee Scale

1. After the performer has assumed the correct starting position, the spotter places her hand on the abdomen. This skill is spotted from the side of the performer.

2. As the legs are raised, the spotter immediately places her right arm around the performer's back and grasps her left hip. The spotter's left hand moves from the abdomen to the right hip. The spotter must actually raise some students in step 2 to avoid placing too much pressure on the shoulder and neck.

3. As the performer places the knees on the beam, the spotter can begin to release the performer. Sometimes the spotter must tell the performer to place her hands on top of the beam and push to raise the shoulders.

4-5. Once the performer is balanced, she raises the left leg. The spotter secures the arm, as noted in step 5. The performer's arms can be either vertically positioned or as indicated in the illustration. For the beginner, the further the hands are from the knee, the easier it is to keep balance, since the base is larger. The more advanced student may prefer the position in the photos, since the smaller base makes it somewhat more difficult.

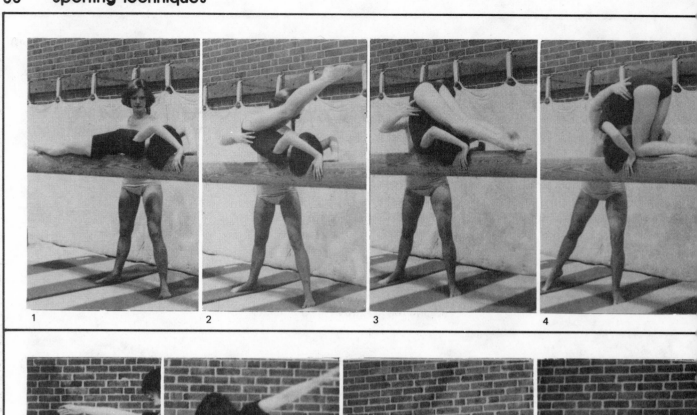

1   2   3   4

1   2   3   4

1   2   3   4

Backward Roll

1. The spotting technique for this skill is very much like the technique just described for the back shoulder roll to knee scale. The spotter should place her left hand on the performer's abdomen or hip.

2. As the hips are raised, the spotter quickly reaches around to grasp the outside hip. Note that the performer has her head on the beam. This is thus a back roll, performed just as one would on the mat.

3. This is the most difficult aspect of the skill. The spotter should lift the hips to relieve the pressure about the arms and neck. Note that the spotter is standing slightly behind the performer and not to her side.

4. As the hips are raised and the arms straighten, the head is free to be raised. The spotter should maintain contact until the skill is completed.

One-Arm Cartwheel

1-2. As the performer gets ready to perform, the spotter raises his left hand. As the performer leans into the skill, the spotter reaches up to contact the hip area. Note that the spotter's right arm is flexed at the elbow and raised up to the head. This arm quickly moves to the performer's left hip the moment she touches the beam.

3. As the spotter contacts both sides of the performer, he must be alert to improper placement of the performer's right hand or left foot.

4. As the foot is placed on the beam, the spotter keeps his hand contact at the hip in case she should start to fall. The left hand is moved from the performer, thus allowing her to extend the trunk.

5. Note that the spotter's right hand is still at the hip. This is necessary until the performer feels completely confident in the newly attained position.

Back Walkover

1. As the performer gets ready to execute the back walkover, the spotter positions herself. Although this skill can be spotted from the side using the same tumbling technique described in chapter 6, it is better to use the one illustrated here. The spotter stands with her back turned to the performer. Her arms are raised to contact the performer's hips. Contact should be made before the performer begins the skill.

2. As the performer arches backward to see the beam, the spotter keeps her right hand at the lower back position to support the performer. The left hand grasps the performer's right arm to help keep the elbows straight.

3. With the aid of upward force from the spotter's right arm, the performer extends her left leg into the inverted handstand position. The legs should be spread as wide apart as possible. This aspect of the skill aids balance by keeping the center of gravity relatively close to the base. The spotter should help the performer gain an appreciation of the importance of hip position and its influence on safety.

4-5. As the right foot makes contact with the beam, the spotter should hold onto the right arm until the foot is properly positioned. The spotter should keep her hands raised in case the performer wants to reach out and contact them for security.

Side Handstand, Half-Turn Dismount

1. The spotter raises the left arm in anticipation of the forward motion of the performer.

2. As the performer reaches to contact the beam with the right hand, the spotter should already have his left hand on the performer's right hip.

3. The spotter has both hands on the performer. When attempting this skill, the performer should be able to maintain the handstand position. Note that the spotter's right hand contacts the performer's left hip to prevent unnecessary forward movement.

4-5. As the performer raises her left hand from the beam and begins an outward rotation of her left side, the spotter assists by aiding her rotation. Note that the spotter's right arm is bent at the elbow in photo 4 to draw the performer toward him or, in effect, away from the beam. As the performer moves to the side of the beam, the spotter continues to provide support with his right arm. His left hand contacts the performer's right forearm to stabilize the inverted position.

6-7. As the performer lands, the spotter removes his right hand from her side. But he keeps his left hand on her right side to ensure a follow-through contact with the performer.

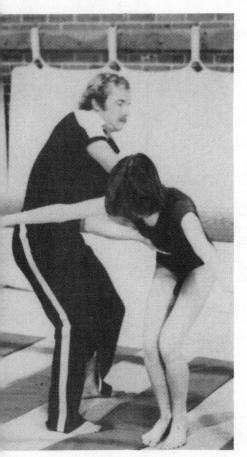

Handstand, Half-Turn, Tuck Dismount

1-2. As the performer leans into the skill, the spotter contacts her right side with the left hand.

3. Once the performer realizes the handstand position, the spotter's right hand contacts her lower back to keep the forward motion in check. The spotter should also inform the performer whether she is executing the skill correctly.

4. As the performer makes the transition from the front handstand to the side handstand, the spotter continues to control the vertical position by exerting reasonable pressure about the hips. Note that the spotter has moved his right hand from the performer's lower back to the left hip.

5. The spotter changes his hand contacts for better support of the performer, and to get out of her way as she begins the tuck dismount. The spotter's left hand will support the performer, as well as help her initiate the backward rotation of the upper body. The spotter's right hand helps the performer maintain the inverted position.

6-7. The performer flexes at the hips and the knees to assume the tuck position. The shoulders should be positioned slightly in front of the beam. If the performer fails to push away from the beam, the spotter will have to lift her.

8. As the performer's feet contact the floor, the spotter can relax to some extent. However, note that his hands remain on the performer in a crossed position.

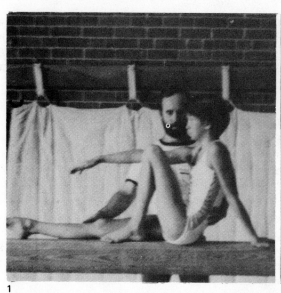

1   2   3

1   2   3   4

1   2   3   4   5

Valdez to Handstand

1. The spotter positions himself beside the performer. His right hand contacts the knee and his left hand is at the performer's lower back. The performer is instructed to raise the hips as high as possible to reach the position in step 2.

2. Note that the performer's upward thrust is controlled by the spotter. His left hand is primarily responsible for movement of the hips up and above the base—the hands. The right hand helps position the performer's right leg.

3. Note that the spotter's left arm is still at the lower back. The right hand is also important, since it is helpful in positioning the hips above the hands. The spotter's pressure on the right leg helps move the hips up and backward.

4. The spotter should be especially careful when the legs are moved together. The more stretched out the performer, the farther the center of gravity is from the base. Here, the spotter's right arm is the primary stabilizer.

5. As the performer drops one foot to the beam, the spotter quickly moves his left hand from the back area to the abdomen to lessen the force of the descent.

Back Walkover to Side Split

1. The spotter assumes the correct position to take the weight of the performer as she leans backward. Note that both of the spotter's hands are raised and make contact with the lower back.

2. The spotter should gradually assume the weight of the performer until her hands contact the beam, as well as help guide the performer to the beam. By extending her own elbows, the spotter raises the performer's center of gravity, helping her assume the inverted position in step 3.

3. The spotter's hands must not slip off the performer at this point. As the hips move past vertical and begin to descend, the spotter must lift against the pull of gravity. At the same time, the performer must direct her right foot between her hands.

4. The spotter should maintain contact with the performer until she has correctly assumed the side split position.

Front Walkover

1-2. When the performer raises her arms above the shoulders, this indicates she is ready to begin the skill. As the performer's arms move toward the beam, the spotter raises his to establish contact just before she touches the beam.

3. The spotter places his left hand at the elbow nearest to him, and his right hand under the performer's left hip. As the performer's left foot moves toward the beam, the spotter should be conscious of whether it is above or to the side of the beam. Naturally, if the foot is above the beam, the spotter should feel confident that the performer will safely complete the skill with his help. However, if the foot is directed toward either side of the beam, then the spotter should either support the performer back to the floor or support her until she positions the foot on the beam correctly.

4-5. As the performer's foot contacts the beam, the spotter should provide additional force with his right hand to raise the performer above her newly formed base. His left hand also helps by assisting with the upward motion of the upper trunk.

1   2   3   4

1   2   3   4

1   2   3   4

Cartwheel Dismount

1. The spotter raises his left arm to inform the performer that he is ready to spot her. The raised position of the arm also aids in the immediate contact needed at the performer's right hip.

2. As the performer contacts the beam with her hands, the spotter grasps both hips, as illustrated in photo 2. The spotter's primary job is to guide the performer over the end of the beam to the mat. His right hand is primarily responsible for controlling the speed of the descent.

3. The spotter should use only the amount of force needed to keep the performer from landing too hard. Note that the spotter leans in the direction of the dismount. The spotter's left hand is responsible for preventing the performer from overspinning.

4. The spotter should have his right hand on the performer's left side, while the left hand remains on her right side. This is often referred to as the *crossed-arm position*. Note that the spotter does not lose contact with the performer.

Roundoff Dismount

1-2. Spotting steps 1 and 2 is essentially the same as spotting for a cartwheel. Remember, however, that the spotter contacts the performer first with the left arm and then with the right. The spotter's left arm aids the performer in assuming the inverted position, while the right arm guides and controls the downward phase of the skill.

3-4. Note that the spotter's right arm is flexed at the elbow to allow the performer to continue with the descent phase. The spotter's pressure at the hip should gradually decrease as the performer nears completion of the skill. The spotter's left hand should maintain contact with the performer's left side to prevent any backward rotation.

Front Handspring Dismount

1. As the performer contacts the end of the beam with her hands, the spotter grasps the right arm just above the elbow joint, with the palm up. To spot with the palm down creates unnecessary problems for the beginning spotter. The spotter's right arm is raised, ready to contact the performer's lower back, as noted in photo 2.

2. The spotter's right hand aids in forward control of the performer. Note that the right arm is fully extended, so the spotter makes contact with the performer as early as possible. Early contact allows for better control of force than if it is made later, in the descent phase of the skill.

3-4. The left arm controls the performer's upper body, preventing any possibility of an overspin. The right arm supports the performer during flight (step 3) and on landing (step 4).

Side Aerial Dismount

1. The spotter raises her left hand to alert the gymnast she is ready.

2. As the gymnast's right foot pushes vigorously to lift the hips, the spotter makes contact with the left hand at the right hip. Note that the spotter's right hand is moving toward the performer's left hip. The spotter's feet are sufficiently wide to enable her to maintain control of the performer.

3. In this photo, note the spotter's points of contact on the performer's hips.

4. As the performer's feet come to rest on the mat, the spotter should have her arms in a crossed position. The spotter's left arm is important, since it helps to prevent the performer from overspinning.

Front Aerial Dismount

1. The spotter reaches forward to contact the performer's abdomen to assist her during the upward phase of the skill. Note the position of the spotter's right arm. As the performer drops her head, this arm can easily be moved in to touch the back or side (step 2).

2. As the performer plantar flexes the right foot and swings the left leg up into the air, the spotter quickly moves the right hand to the back for better control of the descent phase of the skill.

3. The spotter's left arm is on the abdomen, and her right arm is on the back. Note that both arms are flexed at the elbows for better control of the performer.

4. When the performer contacts the mat, the spotter should be in a cross-arm position. The spotter's left arm keeps the performer from overspinning.

Back Flip Dismount

1. Before the performer begins the skill, the spotter should be positioned with her right hand at the lower back area. The contact should be such that the fingers and thumb grasp part of the performer's leotard or shirt.

2. As the performer pushes up into the air and flexes at the hips and knees, the spotter should stay with her. She must never lose contact with the performer. The spotter's left hand assists by providing the force needed to ensure safe rotation, should the performer fail to rotate properly.

3-4. Note that the spotter is leaning in the direction of the performer's landing. You will note that in step 3 the spotter is still grasping part of the performer's leotard. This is important because the back cannot be controlled as easily as the hips. The hips provide something to apply pressure to, thus making the spotting process easier.

1 2 3 4 5

1 2 3 4 5 6

Front Flip Dismount

1-2. As the performer approaches the end of the beam, the spotter quickly reaches upward and places his hand on the right side of the abdomen.

3-4. The spotter's right hand contacts the performer's back to assist during the rotation of the flip, as well as to support the weight of the performer. The spotter's left hand aids the performer first by upward movement, and then by moving across the body to enhance the rotational velocity of the flip.

5-6. As the performer lands, the spotter maintains control by keeping his hands in the positions noted in photo 5. The spotter's left hand prevents an overspin.

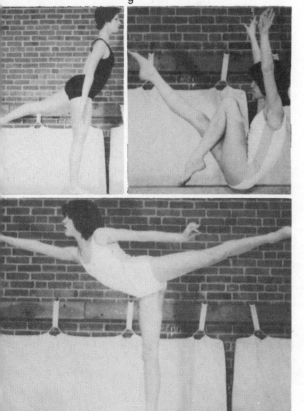

9

Balances and Poses

Any of the following skills can be spotted by simply standing within an arm's reach of the performer. Initially, beginning students will require hand-to-hand contact to build confidence. But after a few attempts, most students will not need a spotter for these skills.

1. Arch Post
2. Deep Front Scale
3. Swan Scale
4. Arabesque en Plie
5. Pose
6. Pose
7. Front Scale
8. Arabesque
9. Single-Leg *V* Seat

8

Uneven Parallel Bars

The uneven parallel bars is an interesting apparatus in women's gymnastics. There are plenty of skills for both beginning and advanced students. Progress by national and international gymnasts will encourage performers to attempt increasingly difficult skills on this apparatus. This is one major reason why gymnastics students must be properly cautioned and supervised during all levels of gymnastics instruction and competition.

The uneven parallel bars was designed during the 1930s to provide girls gymnastics with skills comparable to men's parallel bars. The uneven position of the bars allows the performer the opportunity to exploit her true physical potential more effectively. As a result, the girls who participate in this event generally display considerable confidence and strength.

Very young children (four to six years of age) benefit greatly from the adaptability of the uneven parallel bars. When working with young children in community programs, the spotters must be very good and sincerely interested in the safety of the children. At times, parents may want their child to progress faster than the child is safely capable of performing. Those of us who have been in gymnastics for some years will appreciate that statement. There are, of course, many parents with a serious and sound attitude toward their child's progress. Such parents will respect the spotter's desire to progress only as fast as the child is able, and within the child's individual physical and mental limits. Hence, the spotter should know when to stop introducing new skills to allow the child adequate time to master the fundamentals of the previously taught skills. The performers should also be required to assess their own progress and, in essence, determine how much longer they should continue practicing certain fundamentals.

Although the performer should be responsible for checking the safety of the apparatus before each practice session, the spotter/teacher must assume the major responsibility. Proper care and maintenance of the apparatus is the instructor's job and should be performed regularly. If the instructor notices unsafe supporting devices or bars, they must be corrected or replaced. The safety of the performer should be of utmost importance in the minds of the spotter, instructor, school, or club. The spotter should be especially aware of overlapping mats and any such condition that may complicate a dismount. If possible, the person in charge should obtain the best mats available or, at least, use several mats to increase their thickness and effectiveness in taking up the force of landing.

More specifically, the spotter must know how to spot every skill that the performer attempts, otherwise, unnecessary risk is assumed by the gymnast. When in doubt about the correct hand placement, stop the performer and talk through the progression. The spotter may need to seek assistance from another coach or to take time to analyze another performer's execution frame-by-frame.

In essence, the trained spotter enhances the learning process by providing sound instructions. During this process of mental and physical readjustment, the spotter must continue to protect the performer from falls and bruises. The safety of the performer depends on whether the spotter has a sincere concern for the worth of every young person. This kind of person will pay close attention to the details of spotting techniques. You can become a proficient spotter by paying close attention to the spotters depicted in the sequence photos for the individual skills. You must learn how to use your arms with force and control to work smoothly with the performer. Study the arms and their influence on the direction of specific parts of given skills. Then, examine the position of the feet and legs, since they play a big part in stabilizing both the performer and the spotter. The spotter must have a solid base to spot from if the performer and the spotter are to work together safely.

When necessary, the spotter appears in the photo alongside the performer during the execution of the skill. The descriptions are centered around the role of the spotter, rather than the traditional approach of merely describing the skill. Spotting is a tremendous skill in itself. It requires the same amount of practice and feedback as the execution of a skill by a performer. Only then can you rectify poor habits and build consistency into neuromuscular responses.

1 2 3 4

1 2 3

1 2 3

Back Hip-Circle Mount

1. The spotter places her left hand on the right side of the performer. Note that the spotter has a large base and is leaning in the direction of the performer.

2. As the performer flexes the right hip and raises the leg toward the bar, she is assisted by the spotter via the right hand. While the leg is being raised, it is important for the spotter to continue applying pressure at the lower back to move the hips to the bar.

3. Once the performer's legs are over the bar, the spotter can position both hands at the back to push the hips into the bar. At this time, the spotter should encourage the performer to keep her arms flexed at the elbows so that the upper body remains close to the bar.

4-5. As the performer comes to rest on the bar, the spotter grasps the performer's right arm to aid in the final upward-backward aspect of the skill. The left arm of the spotter contacts the performer's legs to stabilize her in the straight-arm support position.

Flank Vault Mount

1. The right forearm of the spotter supports the performer as she jumps upward to advance over the bar. The spotter's left hand controls the left arm support of the performer if she goes beyond the bar.

2. Note the upward and lateral lift the spotter provides the student.

3. Once the student comes to rest on the bar, the spotter moves his hand to the right hip area to secure the position. His left hand remains in contact with the performer's left hand.

4. The performer's right hand returns to the bar, while the spotter maintains contact with the performer's left arm and right sides.

Front Support to Cast

1. As the performer positions herself in a front support, the spotter contacts the right side of the performer, as well as the legs.

2. As the performer flexes at the hips, the spotter quickly places her hands behind the legs to assist her.

3. During the extension phase, however, the spotter returns the hands to the anterior surface of the thighs to supplement the performer's force.

4. The performer was able to attain the height in photo 4 due to the extension of the hips, the push from her arms, and the push from the spotter. The performer's arms should remain straight as the hips are pressed upward.

1   2   3

1   2   3   4

1   2   3

Back Hip Circle

1. The spotter can stand on either side of the low bar while spotting the back hip circle. The stronger the spotter, the easier it is to spot behind the bar. An untrained or fairly weak spotter should stand in front of the bar. The spotter places her left hand at the lower back area and her right hand at the lateral-posterior aspect of the performer's right thigh.

2. While the legs move around the bar, the spotter maintains contact at the two points previously indicated.

3. The moment the legs begin to move downward, the spotter quickly changes the points of contact. Her right hand moves from the performer's legs to her right arm. At the same time, the spotter's left hand moves from the lower back to the legs.

Back Hip-Circle Mount

1. The performer has reached the position in photo 1 after a few steps of running. First, the performer's hands make contact with the bar. At the same time, the spotter reaches in and contacts the performer. His left hand is at the abdomen, while the right hand helps keep the legs elevated for a short period of time.

2. As the shoulders of the performer begin the backward motion and the legs move forward, the spotter moves his hands from the anterior to the posterior part of the body. Note that the spotter's left hand moves to the back, while the right hand makes contact with the back of the legs.

3. The right hand keeps the hips close to the bar, while the left hand rotates the legs around the bar.

4. As the legs pass vertical, the spotter once again changes contacts. Now, the right hand moves to the legs to stabilize them while the performer finishes the move.

5. Once the legs are stable, the spotter may place his right hand on the lower back to keep the performer from overspinning.

Single-Leg Shoot-Through to Stride Support

1. The spotter places his left hand on the performer's right elbow. The spotter's right hand is placed on the abdomen. At this point, the performer is undergoing the forward travel of the legs to cast.

2. As the legs move backward and upward, the spotter continues to push the hips upward to provide a few seconds of time for the performer to bring one leg in over the bar. But the spotter must not linger too long on the push aspect of the technique, or else the performer's right knee will be prevented from moving forward. As the hips are raised, it is essential that the spotter help keep the performer's shoulders slightly in front of the bar.

3. Once the leg is stretched forward in the stride support, the spotter should contact the abdomen to bring the performer under control. The spotter's left hand maintains contact with the right arm of the performer. Note that the spotter assists the right arm of the performer by simply grasping the arm in front of the bar, rather than going under the bar.

1   2   3   4

1   2   3

1   2   3   4

Hook Swing, Half-Turn, Catch High Bar

1. The spotter places his right hand on the performer's feet. The spotter's left hand should be at the lower back area to aid in balancing on the bar. Before the performer reaches step 2, it is imperative that she straighten the body on falling backward.

2. As the performer sits backward, the spotter moves his left hand from the back to the abdomen to assist during the lift phase. The spotter's right hand remains at the feet to insure that the performer does not extend the legs prematurely.

3. Once the performer reaches a near horizontal position, the spotter changes contact points. The spotter's right hand moves from the feet to the right side of the performer. The left hand shifts from the right to the left side. These changes are necessary to assist the performer properly during the one-half turn part of the skill. That is, to realize the turn and upward motion necessary to grasp the bar, the spotter's left hand shifts toward him, while the right hand moves away from his chest.

4. The spotter's hands remain on the performer to insure that the newly formed position is secure.

Inverted Tuck, Knee-Rise Mount to Stride Support

1-2. The performer uses a tuck to make it easier to get the leg under and over the bar. As the right leg is being positioned, the spotter should support the lower back with her left hand. The spotter's right hand provides an upward force to help the performer lift the legs to the bar.

3-4. As the performer's left leg straightens, the spotter's right hand pushes downward to create the necessary backward and upward motion to move above the bars. If the right knee begins to straighten, the spotting process becomes extremely difficult. So the spotter should encourage the performer to keep the knee positioned tightly around the bar. The left hand of the spotter continues to provide assistance at the back and hip area. Once the performer is on top of the bar, the spotter should maintain contact with the back leg to aid in stabilizing the move.

Front Mill Catch

1. Once the performer has properly positioned herself, with the hands in the reverse grip, the spotter moves to a position behind the bars. He then reaches under the bar and up to grasp the right forearm or elbow of the performer. At this time, he may inform the performer that the front leg should be held above the bar and stretched forward as much as possible. He may also tell her to avoid bending the arms throughout the skill. Make sure that the performer has the correct grip; otherwise she will roll out of the grip and fall. But even if something like this happens, a good spotter should have already acquired a tight grip about the waist, so the head does not contact the floor.

2. The spotter must make as rapid contact with the left arm as possible. The earlier he establishes contact with the back, the easier it is to control the skill. Note also the spotter's slight knee flexion which helps him reach for the performer instead of waiting for her to come to him.

3-4. Just as the performer is about to finish the skill, she must release the bar and catch the high bar. To do this correctly, the eyes must be open and the leg on top of the bar must press downward. The spotter releases the right arm and places both his hands on the back of the performer.

1

2

3

1

2

3

1

2

3

Front Hip Circle

1. The contact points noted in photo 1 are used to stabilize the performer, not to spot the skill. As the performer raises her center of gravity just before falling forward, the spotter stands to the side of her and waits.

2. The moment the forward progression begins, the spotter should reach in with the left hand and contact the back. The right hand should follow closely, making contact with the posterior part of the performer's legs.

3. Note that the legs are supported by the spotter's right hand. The spotter's left hand lifts the hips toward the bar.

4. As the abdomen of the performer comes to rest on the bar, the spotter continues to provide assistance, both physically and verbally.

Back Seat Circle

1. The performer sits on the bar with an overgrip, while the spotter stands in front of the bar. The spotter's left hand is positioned under the bar to grasp the right wrist of the performer. The spotter must make sure that the back of her hand is facing toward her. Therefore, the spotter's little finger must be up, or the progression of the swing will make it difficult to hold onto the wrist. The spotter's right hand is also under the bar. It should be on the abdomen or, at least, on the right side of the performer.

2. As the performer sits backward into the skill, the right hand of the spotter moves vigorously with her to assist in the down and up part of the skill. The spotter's left hand insures safety by keeping the head off the floor, while the right hand aids during the rotation phase.

3. If the upward part of the skill is incomplete or just short of the top of the bar, the spotter can help by pushing up and back with the right hand.

Double-Leg Shoot-Through

1. The spotter stands to the side of the performer, with her left hand at the elbow.

2. The performer can simply raise her hips and place the feet over the bar, or she can *cast* first.* If additional help is needed, the spotter may place her right hand on the performer's abdomen and provide extra force during the cast. If, however, the performer does not want or need the assistance, then the spotting technique indicated is acceptable. The spotter's left hand stabilizes the forward movement of the shoulders as the feet and hips are lifted.

3. As the legs are extended over and beyond the bar, the spotter continues to exert pressure on the forearm or elbow to help the performer maintain balance.

* A *cast* involves flexing at the hips, followed by hip extension, to a point away from and slightly above the bar.

1   2   3

1   2   3

1   2   3

Front Seat Circle

1-2. The performer flexes at the hips and raises her legs from the bar, with hands in the reverse grip position. The spotter stands behind the bar and reaches under to grasp the right elbow of the performer. The spotter's right hand should be positioned with thumb down, little finger up, and back of the hand facing toward him. The purpose of the spotter's contact is to keep the performer's head off the floor should the hands release the bar.

3. As the gymnast nears completion of the forward circular motion, the spotter quickly moves his left hand to her back to assist during the final phase of the skill. This hand helps to keep the body close to the bar, thus enabling the performer to cope with the mechanics of the skill.

4. If too much circular motion propels the performer beyond the top of the bar, the spotter should inform the gymnast to release the left hand and jump to the floor. The spotter should, however, maintain contact with the performer's right hand. Otherwise the performer is likely to reach a resting position on the bar. The spotter can help control this problem by avoiding placing too much pressure on the performer's back.

Straddle Sole Circle, Forward to Kip Position

1. As the performer acquires the position in photo 1, the spotter places her left hand at the performer's right elbow and her right hand on the performer's abdomen. After the performer assumes a small pike and then extends the hips, the spotter applies pressure at both contact points.

2. The right hand of the spotter pushes the performer upward to assist with the upward motion of the hips. The left hand stabilizes this momentary position on top of the bars. At this time, the performer must reverse her grip. The performer begins the forward motion by leaning forward with her shoulders.

3. Once the performer is ready to straddle forward, the spotter moves to the side. The spotter may aid the performer during the bottoming effect by assisting at the lower back area. This type of spot must be extremely fast.

4. After the straddle sole circle is approximately three-fourths finished, the performer releases the bar and grasps it quickly with an overhand grip. This type of grip is necessary to execute, for example, a kip. The performer is then in the correct position to begin the fundamentals of the next skill.

Jump and Glide (Learning Progression for Glide Kip)

1. The performer stands a few feet from the bar so that when she stretches for it her hands will contact it. The spotter stands behind the performer with a hand on each hip.

2. The moment the performer jumps and pikes, the spotter assists by raising the performer's hips. This position is often held for a few seconds to help the performer gain an appreciation for the tight flexion about the hips.

3. After encouraging the performer to maintain the desired leg lift, the spotter may provide a small forward push to assist the full body extension. If the performer has difficulty holding the legs up when they are together, she should try the glide with the legs in the straddle position. The feet should be no more than a couple inches from the mat during the glide.

1   2   3   4

1   2   3

1   2   3   4

Glide Kip

1-2. The spotter stands to the side and slightly in front of the performer. Note the flexion of the performer's hips in photo 1, which precedes the straddle, hip flexion in photo 2. As the performer straddles the legs, the spotter must wait until the performer's legs are under the bar before moving in to spot.

3. As the performer glides forward, the spotter should place his left hand on the back to assist with the final upward thrust of the hips. The spotter must also move to a position under the bar for better contact with the performer.

4-5. After hand contact is made at the back, the spotter's right hand moves quickly to the legs. Both of the spotter's hands aid the performer in moving from the pike position in photo 4 to the straight-arm support position in photo 5. The spotter's right hand must support and control the performer's weight as well as the reactive forces of her legs. His hands should direct the performer's hips to the bar.

Glide Kip, Single-Leg Shoot-Through Mount

1-2. The spotter waits until the performer has completed the straddle glide. Then, as the legs begin to rise, she must quickly move toward the performer. She provides assistance to the lower back and the leg that remains straight.

3. Note that the spotter has her right hand on the posterior part of the performer's left leg. This contact point helps the performer to pull her hips toward the bar, enhancing the upward motion of the right leg.

4. As the performer comes to rest on top of the bar, the spotter's right hand moves to the anterior-medial surface of the performer's knee to stabilize her. The spotter's left hand is still at the lower back or hip area.

Glide Kip Catch Mount

1. In photo 1, the performer prepares to reach for the bar.

2-3. The performer executes the straddle glide without the assistance of the spotter.

4. As the performer flexes at the hips to position the legs close to the bar, the spotter moves closer to her to assist. He places his left hand at the lower back.

5. As the kip is about to be finished, the performer releases the low bar and reaches for the high bar. During this transition, the spotter aids by keeping the legs stable with his right hand, and stabilizing the lower back with his left

hand. Note the full involvement of the spotter's body in step 5, as well as the flexion of both knees and the wide base. These are necessary adjustments if the spotter is to handle adequately the performer's body weight.

6. The spotter should maintain contact with the performer until she is totally in control of the performance.

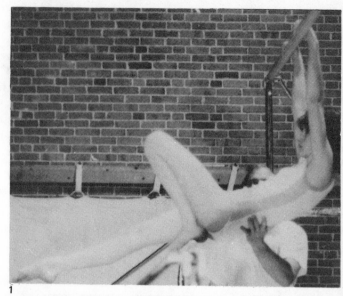

1   2   3

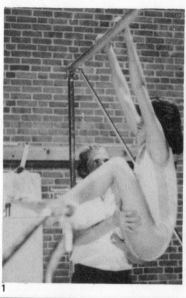

1   2   3

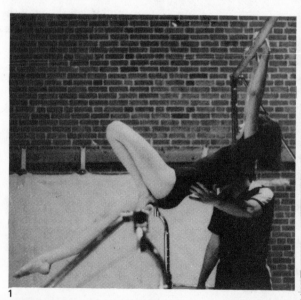

1   2   3

Back Pullover

1. The performer positions herself between the bars by grasping the high bar while supported by the low bar. Note that the right leg is straight, while the left leg is flexed at the hip and knee. The spotter has the left hand at the lower back, and is positioned between the bars.

2. As the performer's right leg is raised, the spotter presses the lower back area to assist with the upward motion. The left leg of the performer also assists through a vigorous extension at the knee and the hip joints.

3. As the hips move closer to the high bar, the spotter continues to press the back of the performer. Note the spotter's two hand contacts: while the left arm helps to raise the body, the right arm pushes the body closer to the bar.

4. Once the gymnast is on top of the bar, the spotter should quickly grasp the legs to insure that any additional angular momentum is neutralized.

Double-Leg Rise

1-2. The spotter contacts the legs with the right hand and the thighs with the left. Just as the performer begins to extend the legs and pull vigorously with the arms, the spotter pushes the performer to the position in photo 2.

3. The spotter's left arm remains raised to stabilize the legs.

Single-Leg Stem Rise

1. The spotter places the left hand under the performer's lower back as she gets ready to lift the right leg.

2. As the performer raises the leg to the top bar, the spotter contacts it (as in photo 2).

3. The performer attempts to keep the right leg close to the bar as she extends the left leg. She must also flex the elbows to pull her hip in close to the top bar. The spotter helps during the extension of the left leg by pushing her lower back toward the bar. His right hand helps her keep the right leg close to the bar. Notice how the right leg has moved above the bar. This is referred to as "pulling the bar down the leg."

4. Once the performer is in the front support position, the spotter maintains contact with the legs.

1

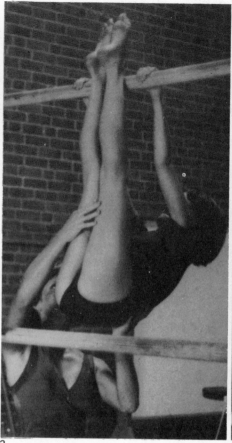

2

3

1

2

3

4

5

Between-Bars Kip

1. The performer assumes the correct body position, with the hands grasping the high bar and hips resting on the low bar. The left hand of the spotter contacts the lower back.

2. Once the legs are raised via hip flexion, the spotter places her right hand on the posterior part of the legs. This contact point helps to draw the legs in close to the chest. The left hand of the spotter serves as a support arm during this part of the skill. However, as the hips move closer to the bar, the spotter's right hand begins to accept most of the burden of supporting the performer.

3-4. As the performer realizes the straight-arm front support, the spotter moves from a two-hand to a one-hand contact. The spotter's raised left arm is an important aspect of this spotting technique. It is the follow-through of the spotting technique, much like the follow-through of a skill.

Front Seat Catch

1. The performer raises from the bar, with the legs straight and the hands in the reverse-grip position. The spotter grasps the performer's right forearm. Note that the spotter's arm is under the bar, with the hand in the thumb down position.

2. As the performer moves under the bar, the spotter should place his left hand under her back for additional support. This contact requires the spotter to flex at the hips and knees. At this point, if the performer loses her grip and moves away from the bar, the spotter should be able to keep the performer's head over the floor as a result of his tight grip at the forearm.

3. Photo 3 demonstrates the effectiveness of the spotter's left hand. By applying reasonable pressure at the back, the performer should be able to complete the circular motion of the legs and upper body.

4-5. As the performer's legs move over and in front of the bar, her hands release the low bar and quickly grasp the top bar. Photo 4 shows the spotter's control of the performer's back as she reaches for the high bar. Once contact is made, the spotter should maintain contact with the performer to ensure a safe grip.

1   2   3

1   2   3   4   5

1   2   3   4   5

Front Sole Circle Catch

1. The performer executes a cast to the position in photo 1. The spotter helps the performer at the beginning of the skill by stabilizing her.

2. Once the forward motion is realized, the spotter flexes at the hips and knees and reaches under the bar to contact the performer as soon as possible. The left hand is at the back, while the right hand is at the legs to insure a safe downward progression of the skill.

3. As the performer moves into the second phase of the skill, the spotter quickly lifts the hips, using the left arm and the right hand. The left arm moves more to the left side of the performer, while the right hand remains at the posterior part of the legs.

4. The performer should thus be able to release the low bar safely and reach for the high bar.

Long Hang Kip

1. The spotter places his right hand at the lower back as the performer moves forward into the long hang position.

2. While the performer moves forward, the spotter pushes the hips upward with the right hand. The spotter's left hand moves to the legs to apply additional pressure.

3. The left hand helps the performer flex at the hips and position the feet close to the bar. The spotter's right hand assists the performer in moving the hips up and forward.

4-5. With a vigorous upward push of the spotter's right hand, the performer moves toward the high bar. The spotter's left hand supports the legs, while the arms remain straight. The left hand provides a base against which the legs can exert pressure, thus aiding upward motion.

6. On completion of the skill, the spotter should remain in contact with the performer.

5. Note the follow-through of the spotter's left arm as he continues to keep his eyes on the performer.

6. As the performer nears completion of the skill, the spotter grasps the right leg to bring her to a complete stop in the straight-arm support position.

Back Hip Circle on High Bar

1. The back hip circle on the high bar is performed the same way as on the low bar. It is imperative that the performer is capable of executing the skill on the low bar before attempting it on the high bar. The increased height makes it more difficult to spot, especially with both arms. So, for safety the performer must thoroughly understand the mechanics of the skill. of the skill.

2-3. Steps 2 and 3 are important aspects of the back hip circle. Photo 2 shows the performer's hips and elbows flexed in preparation for the dynamic backward and upward position in photo 3. Both arms and hips must extend at the same time so there is adequate force to lift the body from the bar. The spotter should be particularly watchful during step 3 should the performer gain too much momentum and start to fall forward of the bar.

4. As the performer's legs and hips return to the bar, the spotter contacts the lower back with his left hand. This insures that the performer's hips will remain close enough to the bar to allow for proper backward motion.

Cut-Catch to Long Hang

1. As the performer sits on the high bar, the spotter holds up his hands in anticipation of the backward motion.

2. The moment the performer sits into the skill, the spotter should contact both sides of the lower back. It is important that the performer allow the hips to complete their forward motion before swinging back toward the spotter. Note that the spotter is standing to the side of the performer so that he can observe the entire skill.

3. After the hips have moved upward toward the bar the second time, the performer quickly releases the bar with both hands and straddles the legs, eventually realizing the long hang position in photo 4. The spotter should support the performer during the release and regrasp of the bar.

4-5. As the regrasp is made, the spotter aids in the necessary backward motion of the hips. Then the spotter's hands release the performer with a quick push of the right hand. This final part of the spotting process is often used to increase the performer's awareness of the hip position relative to the low bar. Such skills as a wrap, wrap half-turn, or a wrap eagle may follow this skill.

Cast

1. The spotters stand on the outside of the bars, with their hands on the performer's thighs and wrists. The performer flexes at the hips and carries out a vigorous hip and elbow extension.

2-3. As the hips are extended and the arms push the upper body away from the bar, the spotters help by supporting the legs. Note that while the spotters support the legs, they maintain contact with the wrist. The performer should begin to feel the correct body position after a few safe attempts.

Cast-Wrap

1. The spotter places her left hand at the legs of the performer to stabilize her.

2-3. As soon as the performer flexes at the hips and begins the cast, the spotter should raise both arms in anticipation of contacting the legs with the left hand and the abdomen with the right. Both hands aid in keeping the performer from hitting the low bar too hard. It is important that the spotter reach up and contact the performer as early as possible for better control of the downward phase of the skill.

4-5. As the performer approaches the low bar, the spotter changes the contact points. The right hand moves to the legs, while the left hand moves from the legs to the lower back. This transition must be very fast for safe execution of the skill.

6-7. After the performer has encircled the bar, the spotter should control any backward rotation of the shoulders by stabilizing the legs. Once the legs are under control, the spotter should place the right hand on the abdomen to encourage the performer to lift the shoulders. It is best to spot this move from between the bars, rather than standing on the opposite side of the low bar. The latter spotting position makes it more difficult to control the cast into the wrap, especially when the cast is horizontal or higher on descending.

Cast-Wrap-Eagle

1. Once the gymnast begins to approach the low bar, the spotter reaches up and contacts her with the left hand at the abdomen and the right hand on the legs.

2. As the hips contact the low bar, the spotter quickly moves his right hand from the legs to the back to push the hips into the bar, while his left hand moves from the abdomen to the legs to push them around the bar.

3. The spotter releases all contact with the performer as she undergoes the wrap. However, during the beginning stages of the eagle, the spotter provides control, with his right hand at the back and his left hand on the legs.

4. The spotter's right hand controls the backward angular motion that is often too great, should the performer flex at the hips.

5. While the right hand helps to create the desired arching effect, the left hand raises the performer if she is too low to grasp the bar.

1   2   3   4

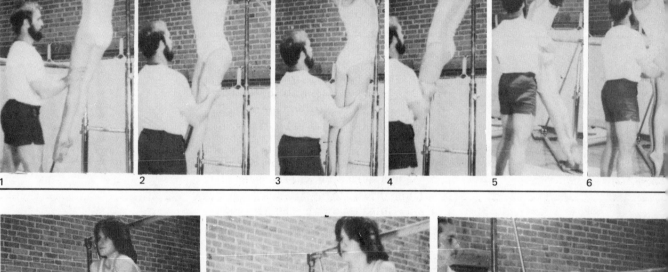

1   2   3   4   5   6

1

2

3

Back-Straddle Catch to Long Hang

1-2. To provide the performer with some confidence, especially during the jump phase over the bar, the spotter should place his left hand on the left leg. This minimal contact lets her know that you are there and ready to spot, though it does not provide any upward pressure.

3. As the performer passes over the high bar in the straddle position, the hands contact the bar. The spotter should hold his hands high in case it is necessary to grasp the shoulders should the performer flip backward.

4. Once the legs are clear of the bar and the performer hangs with the hands, the spotter contacts the thighs to provide the necessary control and hesitation needed for a proper stretch.

5. The spotter allows the legs to move together and then presses the lower back forward, as in photo 5. Such pressure is often necessary to realize the correct body position, if, for example, the performer is going into a wrap. If, on the other hand, the next skill is a drop kip, the spotter should contact both hips and pull the performer toward him to develop the prerequisite hip flexed position.

Back Uprise, Full Twist Catch

1-3. During the upward part of the back uprise, the performer places tremendous downward pressure on the bars with both hands. The spotter contacts the thighs during the uprise to assist the performer as she turns. Note that steps 1 to 3 comprise one-half of the turn. The performer should practice the correct mechanics of the full twist on a tumbling mat and a trampoline before attempting it on the bars. She should also be able to perform a back uprise to the straight-arm position on the high bar as well.

4-7. During the second part of the skill, the spotter continues to help keep the performer's weight under control, while assisting in the twisting process. Once the performer's hands are back on the bar, the spotter continues to contact the waist until he is confident that her grip is secure.

Back-Straddle Seat Circle

1. With the performer in the front support position, the spotter grasps the right elbow with his left hand. His right hand contacts the performer's abdomen.

2. As the performer lifts the hips to straddle over the bar, the spotter pushes the abdomen while maintaining a firm grip at the elbow. The spotter's control of the right support arm of the performer aids her in maintaining balance.

3. As the performer falls backward, the spotter's hands release her. Then as the performer moves under the bar, the spotter contacts the performer's right hip with his left hand to assist with the upward motion.

4. As the performer nears completion of the skill, the spotter quickly grasps the performer's right elbow with his left hand and presses on the abdomen with the right.

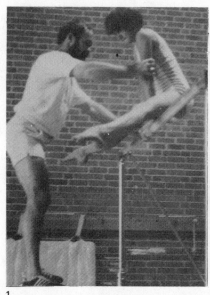

1
2
3

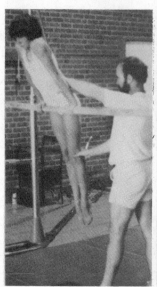

1
2
3
4

1
2
3

Back-Straddle Seat Circle Catch

1. As the performer flexes at the hips and assumes the straddle position, the spotter controls her by contacting her left arm with his right hand.

2. When the backward motion is realized, the spotter must be extremely quick with the right hand. The hand is placed across the abdomen to maintain the desired hip position. The spotter's right hand also helps provide the beginner with the time needed to release the high bar and safely reach for the low bar.

3. Note that the spotter's left arm is in contact with the high bar. The spotter should also insist that the performer keep the legs straight and as wide apart as possible.

4. By flexing the left arm, the spotter moves toward the high bar, allowing the performer to achieve the correct downward position for a safe descent. The spotter's right arm also assists by gradual extension of the elbow, using the forearm flexors.

Front Flip Between Bars

1. While the performer is in the front support position, the spotter places his left hand at left hip and the right hand at the anterior-lateral part of the left knee. Note that the spotter stands between the bars.

2. As the performer's hips are vigorously raised, the spotter aids by pushing the hips upward with the left hand. However, the spotter must move his hand from the performer's hips to her back, as in step 3. The spotter's left hand may appear to be stationary at the performer's chest. But it is actually properly positioned here, before shifting to the performer's back as she moves.

3-4. Once the performer grasps the high bar, the spotter should maintain contact until he is sure the hands are firmly positioned. It is important that the spotter's left hand support the back during the release-catch part of the skill. If the spotter feels uncomfortable spotting this technique alone, then another spotter should stand on the other side of the performer.

Penny-Drop Dismount

1. The right hand of the spotter is positioned over the performer's ankles. The tension must be sufficient to keep the legs from straightening when the performer is inverted. Note that the spotter's left hand is placed on the abdomen. The performer should be encouraged to keep the body straight on releasing the bar.

2-3. The spotter's left hand aids the performer in moving to the position in photo 3. As the performer's body assumes a position horizontal to the floor, the spotter's right hand moves to the lower back.

4. It is imperative to complete the spotting technique correctly. The spotter's left hand must support the performer, while his right hand prevents any possibility of an overspin. Although this is a relatively easy skill, there is always the possibility of overspinning. So, be sure to spot the lower back.

Flank Dismount from Stride Position

1. With the performer in the stride position, the spotter grasps the right arm to stabilize the support, while creating the necessary lateral lean to allow the hips to move above the bar.

2-3. As the performer raises her left leg, her left hand must release the bar. Note that the spotter continues to keep the performer's arm in contact with the bar, especially during the descent phase.

4. As the performer makes contact with the mat, the spotter continues to aid her in case she needs assistance.

Straddle Underswing Dismount from Low Bar

1-2. The spotter helps the performer reach the position in photo 2 by putting pressure on the abdomen. The spotter's left hand grasps the performer's right wrist until the performer begins to descend.

3. Photo 3 shows the performer falling backward in the straddle position. The performer's feet should be positioned close to her hands.

4. As the performer moves under the bar, the spotter grasps the right forearm with his left hand. The spotter's left hand moves from the right arm of the performer, under the bar, and over the right foot to the right arm to maintain contact during the underswing phase.

5. The spotter maintains a tight grip on the right forearm. Note that he moves with the performer's hip extension by rotating his left side and arm toward her.

6-7. While the performer is airborne, the spotter should maintain physical and visual contact. If the performer's arched position is too long or too short just before the landing, it may be necessary to use the right hand to contact the stomach or the lower back, respectively, for a safe landing. Note that the spotter can maintain contact throughout the hip extension phase and landing. This allows for plenty of practice without harm to the performer.

Flank-Cut Dismount

1. The performer sits into the skill by pushing the hips back and downward.

2. As the performer's hips move down and then back up, the spotter should make contact, as in photo 2.

3-4. Once the back and upward motion of the legs and hips is realized, the performer releases the left hand and allows the legs to turn outward. The spotter helps during the first few attempts by supporting the back with the right hand and the legs with the left.

5. On landing, the performer's back should be supported by the spotter. The spotter should encourage the performer to flex at the hips and knees to reduce the force of landing.

Cast-Wrap Hecht Dismount

1. The performer approaches the low bar with a slight arch in the back. This is necessary to reduce the pressure about the hip area.

2. The spotter reaches out to the performer and contacts her abdomen with his right hand and her legs with the left. The left hand is the more important of the two hands at step 2, since it creates the desired angular motion to encircle the bar.

3. Note that the spotter's right hand never leaves the abdomen. In fact, at this time, the right hand aids in the lift part of the skill. The performer should be instructed to lift the upper body vigorously shortly before the position in photo 3.

4. When the performer lifts the shoulders and arms, the force helps to raise the body from the bar. The spotter aids in this process by lifting during the upward and forward phase, using the right arm.

5. The crossed arm position is a must on landing. The right arm will help keep the performer from landing on the floor if the takeoff was made too early. The left arm will keep the performer from overspinning should she come off the bar too late. Finally, the spotter must be dynamic and aggressive when spotting this skill.

Parallel Bars

Skills on the parallel bars are among the easiest and safest to teach in men's gymnastics. One of the reasons for this is that the bars can be adjusted, depending on the height of the student and the skill to be learned. This is not generally the case with the rings or the high bar, although the high bar can be lowered more easily than the rings. The ease of adjusting the bars is also an important factor in spotting parallel bar skills. The height of the rings and the high bar from the floor makes it more difficult to spot either skill.

All beginning performers should progress in a logical fashion with the mastery of the basic skills to allow for a safe progression to more difficult ones. Since the bars are parallel and easily adjustable, the motivated gymnast may go ahead and attempt certain skills without extensive background or the instructor's supervision. Beginning performers should be encouraged to take adequate time in their development to avoid muscular strains and tears around the shoulders and arms. Again, the performer must assume responsibility for his own safety, and respect the need for proper supervision and learning in a logical progression.

Just as one must first learn how to swing before attempting a skill that incorporates a swing (such as the stutz), he must learn the value of working the bars at a low position. By lowering the bars, the force accompanying swing moves becomes less likely to cause damage to the performer.

The spotter and the performer work as a team so the performer can make an unlimited number of attempts without sustaining falls that could be dangerous. While the performer must concentrate on the cues specific to particular skills, the spotter must study the performer's position in flight and intervene only when needed to sustain a particular element of a skill. If the spotter is needed, he must be quick and determined. His movements with the performer must

complement those elements that are reasonably correct, and yet be capable of countering the potentially disruptive forces.

While a major part of the spotter's role can be taught, much as you would teach a forward roll, it takes time before the execution of a given spotting technique becomes an art form. Fortunately, in most class situations spotters do not have to develop to quite this extent. But while it is not essential to the safety of a program, it is certainly desirable. One would hope that the major gymnastic schools, clubs, and teams across the country are led by instructors who are not only competent in spotting, but see the overall need for developing their spotting skills as well as their athletes.

The major concern with spotting parallel bars is the difficulty of assisting the performer without getting the arms caught between the bars and the performer. When hand-spotting above the bars the spotter must always be aware of the possibility of getting his arm caught, and should anticipate the problem. It is his responsibility to avoid the problem—not that of the performer. Whenever possible, the spotter should spot from under the bars.

Pay close attention to the spotting techniques illustrated in this chapter. Note the coordinated movements of the spotter(s) when assisting the performer. Each photo sequence outlines the important step-by-step actions the spotter needs to employ to aid the performer effectively. Skills illustrated without the spotter have explanations to describe the proper spotting mechanics to use if a spotter is present.

The following skills are arranged in the sequence one should use to teach a beginning class on the parallel bars. But realize that a variety of approaches are possible, depending on the level of the students or athletes. Once the basics have been taught, the instructor should introduce intermediate as well as some advanced skills.

L Support

The *L* support is a basic skill performed on the parallel bars. Due to the static aspect of the skill, it can be accomplished without a spotter with no obvious problems. Note that the performer has his legs raised horizontally, the arms are straight, and the upper body is essentially erect. Although this skill seems rather simple, it is actually difficult to perform correctly. The hamstrings must be reasonably flexible to allow full extension of the knee joints. In addition, the abdominal muscles must be tight enough to allow proper position of the pelvic girdle to enhance the contractile power of the hip flexors.

A spotter, if used, would aid the performer in raising the legs to the desired height. The spotter should also inform the performer, both to point the feet if they are relaxed and to position the head forward if it is down.

1

2

3

4

1

2

3

4

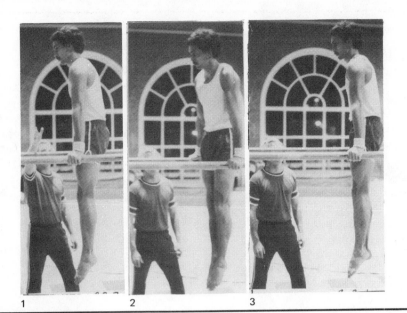

1   2   3

Straight-Arm Walking

1. The spotter stands to the side of the bars while the performer walks down them.

2. Note the forward placement of the performer's right arm to aid continuation of forward motion.

3. As the performer's left arm is placed in line with the right, the spotter raises his hand to conclude the sequence. For heavy performers, it may be necessary for the spotter to help support the legs by grasping them and pushing upward in accordance with the next hand placement.

Forward Straddle across the Bars

1. The performer commences the skill by swinging using the shoulder joints.

2. As the legs are brought forward, they are straddled and stretched across the top of the bars.

3. The hands release and move forward to support the body, as the legs and hips are raised to initiate the swing phase of the straddle forward.

4-5. Note the forward lean of the shoulders as the hips are being raised. The lean is necessary to move the center of gravity closer to the base to ease the body control while raising the hips and legs. The spotter should stand to the side of the bar and be ready to reach in and provide assistance if the performer's arms should bend during the swing phase of the skill.

Single-Leg Cut

1. During the preparatory swing phase, the spotter helps the performer maintain balance after one arm is released by stabilizing the support arm.

2-3. As the right leg is raised over the bar, the performer's right hand must quickly release the bar to allow the leg to cut under and between the bars. As the performer leans forward and laterally to move the center of gravity over the base, the spotter helps keep the arm from bending at the elbow.

4. When the legs are again between the bars, the spotter helps the performer maintain the straight-arm support position.

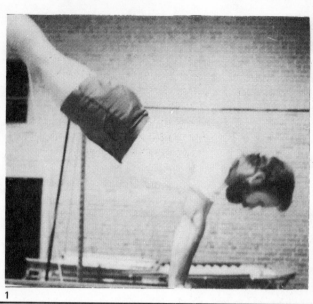

1 2

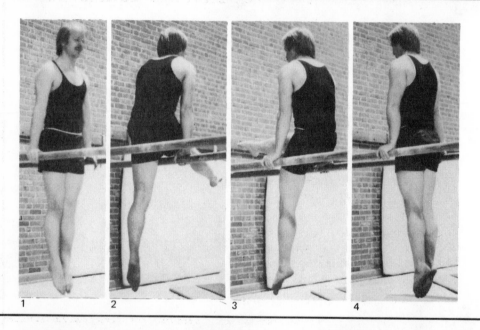

1 2 3 4

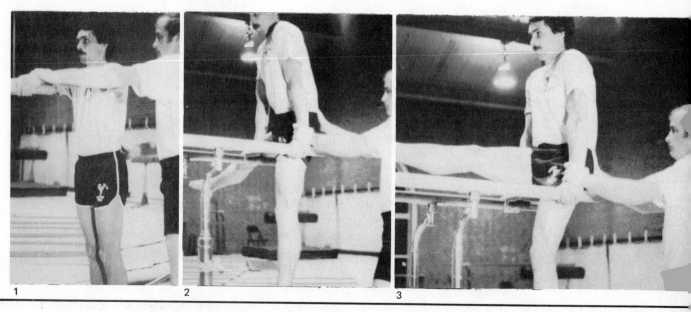

1 2 3

Straight-Arm Support Swing

1. The shoulders are positioned in front of the base (the hands) to keep the center of gravity as close to the base as possible. Dynamic balance is the essence of this skill.

2. As the legs move forward of the base, the shoulders move behind it. This, again, is to maintain dynamic balance by keeping the center of gravity as close to the base as possible. The spotter must help the beginning gymnastic student understand this important concept of movement and control. It may be necessary for a spotter to grasp either the right or the left arm to help maintain a safe swing.

This is a good rule to follow with slightly overweight students or those who may be weak in the upper shoulders. The spotter should encourage the performer to rotate his arms laterally (at the elbow joints) while in the straight-arm support position to lessen the impact on the muscles at the posterior aspect of the arms.

Straight-Arm Support Half-Turn over One Bar

1-2. The performer raises his right leg over the left bar toward his left hand. If a spotter is needed, he should stand to the left side of the performer in step 1, and secure the right arm of the performer as he grasps the bar in step 2.

3. As the right leg comes to rest on the bar, the right hand is also positioned on the left bar.

4. As the right hand gradually assumes more support of the body, the left hand is raised and positioned on the opposite bar. Hence, the performer completes a half-turn in the opposite direction. This skill does not require a spotter.

Single-Leg Cut Mount

1. The spotter places his left hand on the performer's left wrist. The spotter's right hand is placed at the lower back to help raise the hips during the jump toward and over the bar.

2-3. As the performer leans to the left, the right leg is brought over the bar. The right hand is released to allow the right leg to continue forward, as in photo 3. You will also notice that the spotter's right hand is on the performer's back in step 3.

4. Once the right leg is between the bars, the straight-arm support swing is again carried out. The spotter keeps his left hand at the wrist of the performer's left hand in case the skill is not completed correctly.

1

2

3

1

2

3

1

2

3

Double-Leg Cut Mount

1. The spotter places his hands on the performer's hips.

2-3. The performer jumps into the air, releases the bars, cuts both legs over and between the bars, and catches the bars. At the same time, the spotter maintains tight control at the hips. Once the cut-catch mount is completed, the spotter stands to the side and allows the legs to swing backward.

Kip Mount

1. As the performer gets ready to jump into the swing phase of the skill, the spotters place their outside hands at the lower back area.

2. Once the forward pike swing is completed, the spotters make contact with the posterior aspect of the thighs to assist in the upward phase of the skill.

3-4. The performer, keeping his arms straight, eventually rides up, above, and between the bars in a straight-arm support position. The spotters assist during the swing phase—first upward, then forward, and finally upward again to help the performer reach the position in photo 4.

Shoulder Stand

1. As the performer leans forward to position the upper arms on the bars, the spotters help secure the shoulder position. Note that the spotter on the right side has her right arm under the bar pushing upward at the shoulder, while her left hand pulls down on the elbow. Conversely, the spotter on the left side pushes the shoulder upward with his left hand and pulls down on the elbow with his right hand.

2. Once the hips start their forward and upward progression to assume the position in photo 3, the spotters must push upward, as well as pull downward, to help the performer reach the desired position.

3-4. With the hips above the shoulders, and the spotters helping to relieve pressure about the upper arms, the straddle position can be achieved relatively easily. Remember that when the legs are spread, the center of gravity is lowered. But when the performer brings the legs together in step 4, the higher center of gravity makes balance more difficult. Thus, the spotter's role is more important in step 4 than in step 3.

1 2 3

1 2

Front Uprise

1. As the performer begins the forward swing, the spotters place their hands at the back and thighs to assist the performer in extending the elbows. Note that the spotter on the right has his right hand on the back of the performer, while his left hand is at the thigh area.

2. The spotters assist by pushing the performer up above the bars. For maximum stability, the spotters' feet should be fairly wide during the upward phase of the skill.

1 2 3

Back Uprise

1. As the performer approaches the vertical part of the swing, the spotter reaches in, places her right hand at the front of the thighs, and the left hand on the chest. Note that the spotter must stand slightly behind the base of the upper arm swing.

2. Once the back swing is completed, the spotter continues to apply upward pressure to the chest and thighs to assist the performer during extension of the elbows.

3. The final upward thrust of the body is accomplished with the arms straight and the spotter positioned as in photo 3.

2

Upper-Arm Kip to Straddle Support

1. The spotter places his right hand under the performer's back and his left hand on the posterior part of the thigh. The performer's legs should be well above the bars.

2. As the performer extends his arms and thrusts his legs forward, the spotter helps by providing additional force using the contact points in photos 1 and 2.

Upper-Arm Kip to Straight-Arm Support

1. As the performer's legs are raised above the bars, the spotters place their hands on his back and thighs.

2-3. The performer acquires a straight-arm support position by moving the legs upward and forward, while extending the elbows. The spotters help by providing any additional force needed to realize the correct mechanics.

4. As the performer's legs begin to descend, the spotters quickly move their hands from between the bars.

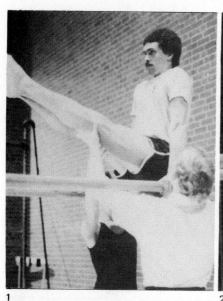
1

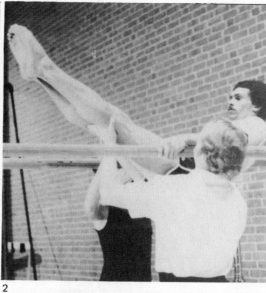
2

3

1

2

3

1

2

3

Cast to Upper-Arm Support

1. As the performer flexes at the hips and begins to fall backward at the shoulders, the male spotter quickly reaches up to contact the back with his right hand and the legs with his left.

2. The second spotter performs the same spotting technique, but in reverse order of step 1. Note that both spotters help maintain the tight hip flexion required for this skill.

3. As the performer's hips and legs descend beneath the bars, the spotters must flex at the knees and hips for adequate reach. As the performer's hips begin to move up and forward,

the spotters will have to extend their legs.

4. In the final part of the skill, the performer moves above the bars into the upper-arm support position. The hand at the performer's back is the most important aspect of spotting in step 4, although the performer's legs must remain in a vertical position.

Cast to Straight-Arm Support

1. The performer's backward descent is spotted by placing hands on the back and the legs (note the female spotter).

2. Since this skill requires considerable force and a powerful upthrust of the legs, the spotting technique must be fast. As the hips move up and above the bars, the spotters contact the back and shoulders to enhance the upward movement.

3. As the spotters continue to support the performer, the performer's arms are positioned to support the body again. Hence, the hands must release

and catch the bars during the transition from step 2 to 3.

Handstand

1. The performer places his hands on the low parallel bars, with his right foot in the swing position. Note that the left leg is slightly flexed at the knee to provide the force to invert the body.

2. By swinging the right leg up while the arms remain straight, the performer attains the handstand position. The spotter should stand to the side of the performer, with an arm across the back to grasp the right hip, while her other hand contacts the performer's left leg. The handstand is generally easier to hold when the legs are spread. The arms should be straight,

shoulders extended, with as little arch in the back as possible.

3. Note that the performer is fairly straight throughout the handstand position. If possible, there should be no arch in the back. The spotter should continue to provide assistance at the hips and legs. When it is time to return to the mat, the spotter helps by providing a small push at the lower back.

1

2

1

2

3

1

2

3

Swing Handstand

1-2. The female spotter positions her right hand so she can contact the performer's abdomen. Thus, she assists the upward phase. The male spotter aids in stabilizing the arms and shoulders. In order to maintain balance, the force used to push the shoulders to a point above the base must equal the force used to invert the body. Hence, the female spotter's role is of great importance. The male spotter contacts the shoulder area with his right hand so the shoulders remain over the base, while his left hand grasps the performer's wrist. Both spotters should be especially aware of the performer's hip and leg position. When it is time to swing down, the spotters should encourage a forward displacement of the shoulders to keep the center of gravity as close to the base as possible.

Bent-Arm Straight-Body Press to Handstand

1. The spotter stands to the side of the performer, with his left hand at the shoulder and the right hand at the abdomen.

2. As the legs begin to move upward, the spotter's right hand assists by helping the body to rotate at the shoulders. Once the legs are semivertical, as they begin to move upward due to extension of the elbows and flexion at the shoulders, the spotter's left hand becomes very important.

3. Once the performer reaches the handstand position, the spotter's hand contacts should be maintained to stabilize the performer.

Two-Arm Handstand into One-Arm Handstand

1. The handstand must be such that the performer is fully confident of his ability to move into and out of the position.

2. The performer attains the straddle hip position.

3. The left hand is slowly removed from the bar. Hence, the right arm and hand of the performer must sustain the entire body weight. The performer should try to keep his right shoulder extended to maximize the intensity of the muscles associated with the right gleno-humeral joint. Also, the abdomen and hip flexors must be tight to keep the legs from moving around. A spotter can be used to make the transition somewhat easier during the first few attempts. The spotter should stand on the one-arm side, with his right hand at the performer's wrist and his left hand at the side of the performer closest to him.

1

2

1

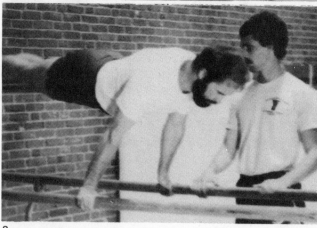

2

3

Straddle Handstand on One Bar

1. The performer usually reaches this position by first performing a regular handstand and then releasing one bar to grasp the other. The spotter spots this move by standing alongside the arm that does not move.

2. As the performer reaches for the other bar, the spotter stabilizes the support arm as well as the back or side with a raised arm.

4

Stutz

1. The spotter stands beside the parallel bars while the performer swings his body several times. Note that the legs are positioned in front of the base—the hands.

2. As the performer moves his legs backward in preparation for the final forward swing, the spotter remains ready until the movement in photo 3 is initiated.

3-4. The performer's legs move forward and attain a reasonable height, while he supports himself using his left arm. The spotter quickly places his right hand on the performer's back to help him during the one-half turn. The spotter's left hand is placed under the thighs to help the performer develop the correct feel for the skill. Note the spotter's final contact points.

Forward Pirouette

1. To perform a pirouette out of a handstand, one must be able to hold the handstand without complications. The body should be extended as straight as possible to complement the turn, as an arched position distracts from the one-half turn.

2-3. The spotter stands to the right of the performer. As the performer's left hand is placed on the bar, the spotter should grasp the wrist with his left hand. Since the performer must push with the left hand to displace the body forward of the right hand, some of his body force must be controlled. The upward motion of the spotter's hand to the abdomen aids in maintaining the inverted position. As the left hand becomes the support arm, the right hand releases and shifts to the other bar. The shoulders should be extended and the body should be as straight as possible.

4. The second handstand is spotted the same as the first, except that the spotter has his hand on the performer's abdomen. The performer should practice the pirouette on the floor and on low parallel bars before attempting it on the high parallel bars.

Peach Basket to Handstand

1. The performer jumps vertically to increase the distance through which the center of gravity travels. The greater the distance, the greater the force. The spotter stands alongside the bars, ready to move in the direction of the skill.

2-3. As the performer swings forward, he pikes to increase his angular velocity. As long as the hands remain in contact with the bars, the performer can put force into the extension-ride phase.

4. The spotter should be ready to contact the performer's chest and abdomen, as well as to push the performer upward. If the spotter detects that the performer is overrotating the skill, he should grasp the performer's shirt at the chest or abdomen and stop the rotation.

5. The airborne phase of the skill should be commenced when the body is positioned above the bars, with no hand contact. The spotter should push the performer vertically upward.

6-7. As the performer's hands contact the bars, the triceps brachii (the muscles at the posterior part of the arms) contract vigorously to control elbow flexion and to extend the elbow joints. The spotter continues to exert pressure on the performer's chest. In order to reach the position in step 7, the shoulders must undergo flexion of the muscles about the gleno-humeral joints. The press phase of the skill is important if the performer is to reach the handstand. The higher the ride-and-regrasp phase, the less the performer will have to press out of the positions in steps 5 and 6. The performer must be strong enough to press the body vertically upward.

1   2   3   4

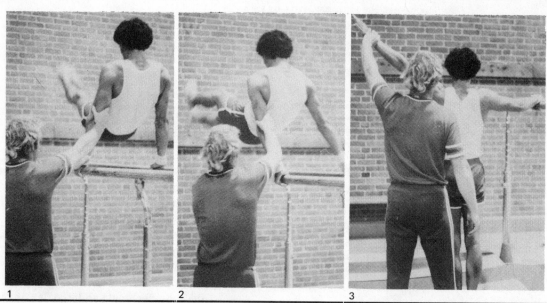

1   2   3

1   2

Front Dismount

1. The performer straightens the body during the front swing.

2. As the legs move back and upward, the performer's shoulders should be slightly forward of the hands.

3. When the legs reach the top of the backswing, the left hand releases the bar and moves to a position just in front of the right hand. The legs should remain together and straight.

4. A lateral push with the performer's left hand aids in continuing body movement to the right of the bar. On landing, the left hand should maintain contact with the bar. With few exceptions, spotting is unnecessary. Should spotting be required, the spotter may stand in front of the performer and assist during the descent phase.

Rear Dismount

1. As the performer's legs move forward and over the bar, the spotter supports the left arm at the wrist and the elbow.

2. After the performer releases the bar with his right hand and the legs move laterally, the spotter must move with the performer.

3. On landing, the performer should keep his right hand on the bar.

Single-Leg Cut Dismount

1. The spotter contacts the performer's left arm during the front swing. As the legs move down and back, the performer will begin to flex at the hips.

2. By raising the hips and leaning to the left, the performer is able to cut his right leg over and around the end of the bar. As his right hand releases the bar, the spotter must secure the left arm and perhaps provide a little lateral and forward pull to position him slightly in front of the bar.

3. The spotter's right hand remains at the wrist, while the left hand releases the arm to support the abdomen should it be needed.

1   2   3   4

1   2   3   4

Double Rear Dismount

1. Since the performer's legs must pass over the right bar, the spotter contacts the lower back area and assists during the lift of the hips. (See step 2.) The spotter's left hand remains on the left arm of the performer.

2. As the performer releases the bar with his right hand and cuts both legs over the bar, the spotter continues to help lift the hips. The spotter's left hand can provide a small lateral lean of the shoulders to help the performer clear the bar.

3. As the legs clear the bars, the spotter provides a small push at the hips to help the performer stand up.

4. Once the performer dismounts, the spotter must move quickly to the side.

Front Flip

1-2. The spotter places his left hand at the wrist of the performer, while his right hand grasps the right shoulder. As the performer raises his hips and pushes vigorously with his arms against the bars, the spotter must quickly raise his arms to help the performer get as high as possible. Raising the arms provides some rotational spin. (See photos 3 and 4.)

3-4. As the performer pushes to his right and passes over the bar, the spotter helps him maintain the desired height until the feet have rotated below the upper body. The performer's left hand moves to the bar nearest his body to help during the landing and the final aspect of the flip.

5. It is important that the spotter maintain contact with the right wrist.

10 Rings

The rings are an exciting event to work, particularly because strength is a tremendous part of these skills.

The importance of strength, when attempting to work the rings, cannot be overemphasized. If the performer lacks sufficient strength to control the body during swinging moves, he may be susceptible to uncontrolled falls and, in general, poor performances. Therefore, all beginners should plan to dedicate part of their workouts to strength training. This should be applied to physical education classes, as well. Performers need to be strong to help each other. By practicing properly with adequate safety guards, the performer will become more efficient in using his muscular strength. His moves will become less jerky and energy absorbing, as the neuromuscular system undergoes minute adjustments.

While strength is important, one must learn how to adapt strength, whether natural or developed through some other sports activity. Weight lifting is an excellent way to become stronger, but the increase in strength may only aid the performer minimally. This means that the stronger students will generally stand a better chance of learning ring skills, assuming they receive adequate instruction and practice the skills enough. This approach reinforces the concept of specificity of training. In simple terms, we become better at those things we practice. So while it is possible to transfer skills from one sport to another, one must expect to work at systematic and dedicated practice to be an all-around performer.

The performer's grip on the rings must be sufficiently powerful to control his body weight and its generated forces. The anterior forearm muscles, responsible for closing the fingers and making a fist, must be strong. The muscles around the shoulders must also be developed. When working with a beginner, regardless of age, the spotter should help reduce the pressure about the shoulders. The spotter should also inform the beginner of any needed adjustments in specific aspects of his performance.

The spotter must never assume that the beginning performer is under control, especially during the first eight to ten attempts of a given skill or sequence.

Spotters should stand to the side of the performer with hands raised. If possible, the spotter should maintain contact with the performer. The spotter should talk to the performer to encourage correct body position, tightness of muscles, and any other factors that may help prevent a fall. Above all, remember that even the simplest moves can be dangerous if the performer does not understand the correct body actions. For example, the performer may raise his legs between the rings in the inverted position to skin-the-cat too quickly, while the legs remain straight on the descent phase. The downward and backward rotating forces may then be sufficient to cause the hands to release the rings. One possibility is that the rotational momentum could carry the feet upward, thus positioning the performer in such a way that he would land on the back or the neck region. All skills must be treated with respect to help ensure the safety of the performer.

To help avoid the above problem, many instructors and coaches feel compelled to reduce the height of the rings during the beginner's initial practice sessions. This is often desirable, since it allows the performer to practice certain moves that would basically be impossible otherwise. Moreover, by lowering the rings, the performer may feel more at ease and thus may concentrate more on correct form.

There must always be an adequate number of mats to reduce the force of landing and the danger of falls. The thickness of the landing mats should be increased as the skills become more advanced. For example, when attempting swinging moves, you should anticipate the ever-present possibility of the performer's hands being pulled off the rings. The moment of greatest danger appears to be when the performer's body moves under the rings. At this point in the swing, the body begins to increase in angular velocity, which may cause the hands to release the rings. The spotter should anticipate this possibility and help the performer make the swing as smooth as possible, or tighten his grip if necessary.

The following skills demonstrate the order the skills should be presented to the beginner, as well as the spotting techniques unique to each skill.

1   2

1   2   3   4

1   2   3   4   5

Pull to an Inverted Position

1. The performer jumps to the rings and pulls himself to an inverted position by flexing the elbows and extending the gleno-humeral joints. The spotter stands to the side of the performer in case the hands should slip from the rings.

2. As the performer's shoulders move backward to allow the body to begin rotation, the spotter may, if necessary, place his hand under the back to assist the performer in reaching the inverted position in photo 2. Note that the performer has his head up so that he can see his feet. He may also rotate the head the other direction so that he can see the floor. The spotter should not take the inverted position lightly. When the performer is inverted, the spotter's hands should be placed on the back or shoulder to insure that the performer will not land uncomfortably should his hands slip from the rings.

Muscle-Up to Straight-Arm Support

1. The spotter supports the performer at the legs while he attempts to grip the rings correctly (using the "false grip").*

2. Since the performer must pull himself to the rings before making the transition in step 3, the spotter must supply the necessary upward push, using the leg contact. The spotter should encourage the performer to keep the rings as close to the body as possible.

3-4. Once the rings are at chest-level, the performer must then extend the arms and flex the shoulders to acquire the position in photo 4. The spotter must be sure that the performer does not assume the straight-arm position without proper spotting. It is possible for the performer to overreact and expend too much energy in the straight-arm support, actually flip himself out of the rings. Contact at the legs is essential for avoiding such an occurrence.

* To attain the "False grip," the performer positions the rings in the heel of the hand, so that each ring runs diagonally across the palm to the big knuckle of the index finger. When the grip is properly attained, the back of the hand faces backward.

Skin-the-Cat

1-2. As the performer begins to flex the hips and knees to position himself as noted in photo 2, the spotter contacts the lower back to provide some additional upward force.

3. Once the legs begin to descend, the spotter should help control the rate at which the legs move downward by placing his left hand at the upper back.

4-5. The performer straightens the legs and allows the hips to move below the rings. The spotter continues to keep his right hand on the shoulder. The performer can then release the rings and drop to his feet, or else flex the hips and knees again and rotate back through the inverted position to step 1.

1 2 3 & 5 4 & 6

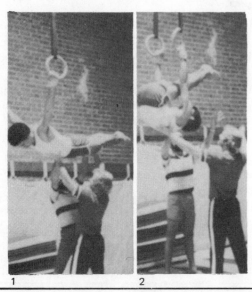

1 2

1 2 3 4

Swinging

1. The pike inverted position should be aided by the spotter. Note that both hands are used to stabilize the performer.

2. As the hips are extended, the spotter continues to maintain contact with the performer. However, once the legs move past the rings, the spotter should not exert any pressure at the back with the right hand.

3. The swing downward should be such that the hips remain straight while the arms move first outward and then over the shoulders. The spotter stands to the side of the performer, ready to contact him should the hands slip from the rings.

4. The back should be arched during the swing. Note that the rings are positioned almost directly over the shoulders.

5-6. Here, the performer repeats the swing as in steps 3 and 4. The performer repeats the same body movement while the spotter stands to the side.

7. During the upward phase, the performer pulls down on the rings to position the body in more of a vertical plane before releasing the rings. The release and landing is made easier if the spotter contacts the abdomen and back of the performer.

Dislocate

1. While the performer is inverted, the spotters each place one hand on the back and ready the other to contact the legs during the descent (in step 2).

2. The moment the performer extends the hips and straightens the body, the spotters reach upward to contact the chest-abdomen and the legs to position the performer correctly and to control the downward motion of the legs. This skill must not be treated lightly by the **gymnastics teacher. If the dislocate is** too low, there may not be enough time to take up the downward force adequately. Hence, the hands could be torn from the rings just as the legs begin to move ahead of the perpendicular. So, all beginners should be spotted during the downward as well as the upward phase. If the hands should release the rings during the upward phase, the performer's body would be directed toward the floor on the neck and shoulders.

Back Kip to an L Support

1. Once the performer acquires a "false grip," he brings his legs up between the rings. Note that the performer flexes slightly at the elbows during the inverted pike position to enhance his strength. The spotter stands to the side and somewhat under the performer. Note the spotter's hand contacts in photo 2.

2. As the performer rotates his hips up and backward, the spotter provides some additional upward force. If the performer is having difficulty with this skill, the spotter should position himself higher and closer, so he can provide more force and control. It is also possible to lower the rings when necessary to help the performer who is not very strong or is slightly overweight.

3. Backward movement of the shoulders, with a straightening of the arms, helps the performer to acquire the position noted in photo 3. If the performer is not strong enough to keep himself in the rings and his arms bend, the spotter should be close enough to help him down safely.

4. The performer assumes the *L* support position by raising the legs to a horizontal position, while the upper body remains essentially vertical to the floor.

1 2 3 4 5

1 2 3 4

1 2 3

Front Roll

1. With the performer in the straight arm support position, the spotter looks on. Note the folded mats, which allow the spotter to get closer to the performer.

2. The moment the performer begins the forward motion by flexing at the hips and elbows, the spotter's left hand contacts the back to lessen the effect of gravity on the elbow flexors.

3. As the performer's back becomes horizontal to the floor, the spotter should contact the back with both hands. The spotter should provide an upward push with the arms to help complete the rotation (refer to photo 4).

4-5. Completing the forward roll requires considerable muscular strength to keep the shoulders moving around the rings. Note that to complete the front roll, the shoulders should move out in front of, under, behind, in front of, and finally above the rings.

Back Roll

1-2. As the performer acquires a "false grip" and lifts the legs, the performer moves noticeably backward. Since the weight of the body is always directed downward, the upper limb muscles must have adequate strength to maintain the correct body position. The spotter helps to relieve the pressure on the arms and chest by placing the left hand at the back and right hand at the legs.

3-4. As the performer's legs lift upward between the rings, the spotter quickly places his right hand under the chest to help raise the upper body. The spotter's left hand supports the legs. Note that in this case as well the spotter stands on several mats to reach the performer more easily.

Back Uprise

1. If the spotter places his right hand at the performer's lower back, the piked inverted position is easier to maintain.

2. As soon as the legs are raised and the hips are extended, the spotter moves his right hand to the abdomen. The earlier the contact the better the spotting technique.

3. Once the legs have reached a near horizontal position, the spotter may, if necessary, use his left hand to keep the legs moving upward. The performer should at least acquire the body position in photo 3 before pulling the arms in to the sides of the body.

4. The spotter should help control the straight-arm support position with his hands until the skill can be performed without complications.

1   2   3   4

1   2   3   4   5

Back Lever

The performer usually attains the back lever position by pulling himself to an inverted hang. Then, as the legs and hips are straightened, the spotter moves in to help support the abdomen and legs. The position in the picture should be maintained for a few seconds, followed by a rest period, and then repeated again. The spotter should be able to gradually release the performer as he acquires the correct feel for the specific muscles involved.

Front Uprise

1. A vigorous push from the spotter helps the performer's legs swing forward. The contact is made while the legs are just past vertical. Note the upward motion of the spotter's hands during step 2.

2. The push provided by the female spotter has aided the performer in attaining the relatively high hip position.

3. Once the hips are elevated, the performer must quickly pull the rings backward, causing the shoulders to move forward and hence over the hips. Forward movement of the shoulders is made easier due to stabilization of the hips and legs by the male spotter.

4. The spotter reaches upward in order to maintain contact with the performer's legs. In so doing, he also **helps the performer to perform the** *L* support.

Inlocate

1-2. While the performer is inverted, the spotters stand as close as possible in case the hands slip from the rings. Note that the female spotter changes her arm position in anticipation of the performer moving closer, and with the need to make an early contact.

3-4. As the legs pass vertical, the spotters contact the performer at the chest and legs. Here, the female spotter provides most of the upward pressure at step 4. Note that her right hand maintains contact with the performer.

5. After the performer rolls his hips over his shoulders (i.e., a forward roll), he comes to a rest in the inverted (or basket) position. Again, the spotters contact the lower back area to stabilize the performer.

Front Lever

The front lever is spotted with the hands contacting the legs and lower back. The spotter pushes upward with a force sufficient to allow the shoulder extensors to acquire the correct hand/hip relationship. That is, the front lever is held only when the center of gravity is positioned directly under the performer's hands. The performer often spreads (abducts) the legs while attempting to hold the front lever, since this moves the center of gravity closer to the upper body. Hence, when the legs are together, the center of gravity is further from the upper body. This makes the skill more difficult. A good spotter can help make the transition from abducting the legs to bringing them together.

1   2   3

1   2   3

1   2   3

Supported "Cross" Position

1. The performer positions himself in the rings, while the spotter supports the feet and legs.

2. As the performer moves his arms outward from his body, the spotter should push upward to help the performer's adducting muscles as they work against the effects of gravity.

3. The "cross" position involves the arms fully straight and horizontal. The spotter, at this point, shares a large part of the performer's weight. Hence, note the flexed position of the spotter's knees and hips, as well as the wide stance.

Bent-Arm Straight-Leg Press to Shoulder Stand

1. From the L support position, the performer pulls the rings in close to the hips. The spotter watches in case something happens that should require his support.

2. The performer flexes at the elbows, allowing the shoulders to move forward of the hands, but close to them. While the forward motion of the upper body is occurring, the hips are also moving up and forward. Note that the legs remain straight during the transition of the hips from the L support to the position in photo 2.

3. As the shoulders become more stable, the hips are slowly extended. Thus the feet, hips, and shoulders make a straight line. The head is slightly extended to enhance the visual aspect of the skill. The spotter continues to look upward in case he should be needed. If necessary, the rings may be lowered to improve contact between the spotter and performer.

Bent-Arm Straight-Body Press to Shoulder Stand

1. The performer is in the L support position. The spotter raises his right hand to stop the motion of the rings.

2. As the legs move downward via hip extension, the spotter provides some force to lessen the inertia of the movement.

3. The performer's shoulders must move in front of the rings as the legs move upward. The downward motion of the shoulders is controlled by the elbow flexion (by the triceps brachii). Once the inverted position is attained, the spotter helps by stabilizing the performer.

1   2   3

1   2   3   4   5   6

1   2   3

Straddle-Leg Press to Handstand

1. With the spotter below the rings, watching should the performer's hands slip from the rings, the performer attempts to maintain the inverted position.

2. To help maintain balance while the elbows are extended, the performer places his feet against the straps. The increased surface area helps to neutralize raising the center of gravity from the base (the rings).

3. As the performer straightens his arms, his feet move closer to each other until they touch.

Dislocate to Shoulder Stand Position

1. The performer pulls himself to the inverted position.

2-3. The performer moves his legs toward the chest, and then vigorously extends his hips, as in photo 3. The spotter stands to the side and provides physical assistance should the performer need it.

4. As the performer's legs move upward, the spotter may provide some additional support if needed.

5-6. The performer in photo 5 is in the shoulder-stand position, with the legs spread to increase stability. When the performer feels comfortable with the position, he moves the legs together.

Handstand

1. The spotter positions himself so that he can contact the right ring and strap for control. The performer has his arms fully extended. His legs are straight, but in contact with the straps.

2. Note that the performer has released the left ring strap with his left foot, while the right foot remains in the same position.

3. The handstand is fully realized once the feet are between the straps. The arms must remain straight. The rings should remain under the shoulders, without excessive motion.

1   2   3   4

1   2   3

Dislocate Straddle Dismount

1. The performer pulls himself to the inverted position. The spotters stand to the side of the performer should the performer need their help.

2. The inverted preparation for the hip extension part of the dislocate is shown in photo 2. Again, the spotters stand to the side of the performer and observe.

3-4. The performer should be able to perform the dislocate to straddle dismount before attempting, for example, the dislocate back flip (tuck, pike, or otherwise). Note that as the performer's legs move closer to the rings, the spotters react by raising their arms in readiness to grasp the hips in step 5.

5. The spotters facilitate the landing by contacting the hips to lessen the force of impact.

Back Flip Dismount

1. During the upward motion of the skill, the performer should try to pull the rings back and away from his legs to avoid contact with the rings. The spotters reach up to contact the performer at the lower back. Note that both of the spotters are fairly close to the performer.

2. Once the performer begins to come out of the tuck, the spotters usually allow the performer to continue the skill. Both spotters, however, have their arms raised to reach in and catch the performer should it become necessary.

3. The spotters contact the hips and lower back to allow for a fairly easy landing.

11

High Bar

The gymnastics student usually looks on high bar skills much the same way as ring skills. That is, they are fun, challenging, and generally more difficult to perform than, for example, parallel bar skills. And like ring skills, high bar skills are generally performed without a spotter in direct contact with the performer (which is generally not the case with parallel bar skills). Both the student and the gymnast must accept this fact, and progress accordingly with the skills.

Spotters can be used for high bar work if the bar is lowered or if a mat (or some type of a standing apparatus) is used. For most of the basic skills, the bar should be lowered (as in many of the following illustrations). Intermediate and advanced skills require that the spotter provide assistance. The spotter can stand either on a folded mat or on an apparatus to contact the performer; or he can stand under the bar or along the mat where the skill concludes (as in a dismount).

Since this book is aimed primarily at physical education classes in gymnastics, the use of an overhead spotting belt is somewhat questionable. In fact, a coach would be likely to use a spotting belt only during certain types of dismounts and giants. When possible, the teacher should emphasize the hand-to-body spotting approach, since this method places the spotter in contact with the performer.

Students must respect the height factor when working high bar skills. The greater the distance from the floor, the more uncomfortable the landings can become. This is certainly a strong reason for not allowing students to play around with high bar skills.

The instructor should also alert spotters to keep an eye on students who display more than an average amount of anxiety when asked to work the high bar. Such students should not be pushed into performing until they are psychologically ready. This is especially true since this particular event demands full coordination between the performer's mind and body. When either the body or mind is less than desired, beware of potential problems. An individual who does not have the strength to hold on to the bar should be spotted every time he grasps the bar. Likewise, when an individual is reluctant to perform given skills, do not rush him.

The beginning performer must progress slowly to avoid unnecessary muscle strains and tears. The hands also require a reasonable amount of time to adjust to the bar. Students should be encouraged to develop a list of skills that they would like to perform. They should be realistic and expect to spend a considerable amount of time preparing for the more difficult skills. As each skill is learned, however, the student (or gymnast) should formulate a routine so that he will gain additional physical stamina.

The spotter, whether a student or teacher, should always check the high bar apparatus and landing mats before each teaching session. He should never assume that the apparatus is secure from one day to the next. In addition, it should be a common practice for the spotter to note whether the performer has either too little or too much chalk on his hands. The spotter should be able to evaluate the performer's grip as to whether it is too loose or too tight. He can also observe the swing of the initial skills to determine the skill level of the performer. The spotter should notice whether the performer appears overly anxious, awkward, and overreactive while performing. The speed of the routine should be evaluated to determine whether the student will have sufficient energy to finish the performance. Lastly, the spotter should note any changes in the eyes or expression of the performer. If the performer appears scared, the spotter should immediately step closer to him.

The reader should realize the ever-present need of the spotter to be active and ready to assist. This is not possible unless the spotter adopts a positive, sincere attitude toward anticipating problems. And, of course, much of one's ability to anticipate problems develops from long hours of intense spotting practice. The beginning spotter, however, can be encouraged to hasten the process through proper verbal cues.

Skin-the-Cat

1. The performer jumps to the bar and allows his body to stretch out in what may be referred to as a long hang position.

2. By flexing the hips and knees while the gleno-humeral joints are extended, the performer's body is positioned with the knees slightly above the abdomen and under the bar.

3. Through continued shoulder extension, the performer's body rotates past the inverted position. If a spotter is used during the performance, he should be positioned beside the performer with a hand under the shoulder. When in doubt whether a spotter should be used, always use one and maybe two (especially when the performer is overweight or deficient in muscle strength).

4. As the legs and hips move closer to the floor, the shoulder joints approach maximum hyperextension. Note that the performer uses the overgrip throughout the skill. By applying a little pressure against the chest, the performer's hips will drop directly over the feet the moment the hands release the bar. The performer can also reverse the skill as well.

Swing

1. The performer usually begins the swing by doing a modified chin. As the legs are raised using hip and knee flexion, the shoulders move backward to enhance the forward thrust of the lower limbs.

2-3. Pushing the legs and hips up and outward provides part of the initial front phase of the swing. The extension of the arms also helps in pushing the body forward.

4-6. Steps 4 and 5 demonstrate the backward phase of the swing. The spotter should stand to the side of the performer and under the bar. The spotter should help the performer understand that the back swing phase causes the grip to loosen, while the front swing tightens the grip. The performer should be instructed to dismount the bar by flexing the elbows to facilitate a vertical descent to the mat. The release and descent to the mat must be accomplished during the back swing.

1   2   3

1   2

1   2   3   4   5

Back Hip Circle

1. During the cast from the bar, the spotter reaches upward to contact the performer at the abdomen and thighs. The contact should be made as early as possible before the performer's trunk makes contact with the bar.

2. As the legs move under and around the bar, the spotter applies pressure at the lower back using the right hand, and at the thighs with the left hand.

3. On completing the backward circle, the performer keeps the legs straight and finishes in a front support. The spotter helps the performer come to a stop by grasping the legs with the right hand and the forearm with the left.

Single-Leg Rise

1. After the performer brings his right leg in under the bar, he flexes the knee around the bar. The left leg remains straight. The spotter stands to the side of the performer, with her left hand on the left thigh and the right hand at the lower back area.

2. The spotter helps position the performer above the bar by pushing down and then up with the left hand and upward with the right. Of course, the performer can acquire the same position by himself by swinging the left leg down and back while pulling in with the arms.

Seat Rise

1. The spotter places his left hand on the performer's thighs and his right hand on the back.

2. As the hips are extended, the spotter places his right hand under the performer's shoulders to enable the performer to flex the arms.

3. Once the hips are positioned above the bar, the spotter's right hand becomes more essential than the left. The spotter must provide the necessary force to rotate the performer to the position in photo 4.

4. Note the vigorous use of the spotter's right hand and arm. The left hand helps control the legs.

5. The sitting position is the final phase of the seat rise. The spotter has his right hand at the performer's left elbow, while the left hand remains on the legs.

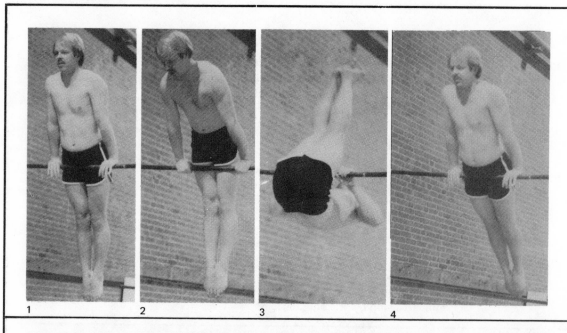

1   2   3   4

  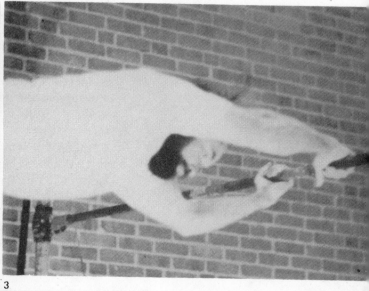

1   2   3

1   2   3   4   5

Front Hip Circle

1-2. The spotting technique for the front hip circle has already been described for the uneven parallen bars in chapter 8. However, should a spotter be used for this skill, he should stand to the side of the performer. If the spotter stands to the left side, he should use the right hand to support and rotate the back while the left hand supports the legs. Note that the performer has raised himself to a thigh position. This upward and forward displacement of the upper body aids in developing the necessary momentum to circle the bar.

3. Once the upper body starts around the bar, the elbows flex to draw the bar in closer to the abdomen. This phase of the skill must be performed extremely fast.

4. In the final step, the performer returns to the same position as in step 1.

Straddle Sole Circle Half-Turn

1. The performer positions himself in a front support.

2. After vigorous flexion of the hips, with a high cast, the performer positions his legs so they can be placed on the bar as indicated in photo 2. Once in the straddle sole position, the hips are displaced backward in preparation for the down and upward phase.

3. When the hips have reached their maximum height, the feet release the bar and move up and outward. As the legs come together, the performer must release the bar with his right hand, undergo a one-half turn, and regrasp the bar as indicated in photo

3. The final grip is called the "mixed grip"; that is, the performer has one hand (palm) down and the other palm up. An easy way to spot this move is to stand on the side on which the half-turn occurs. As the performer's hips move toward the spotter, the spotter should contact the abdomen with the right hand and the thighs with the left.

Back Uprise

1-3. By flexing and extending the hips and arms, the performer acquires a high swing to increase the distance through which force can be generated. The spotter helps by pushing the performer's hips up and forward.

4-5. During the back swing, the spotter contacts the performer's thighs to assist in raising the hips to the bar. For beginners, the spotter should provide sufficient upward pressure at both the chest and the legs to reduce the resistance often experienced during the first few attempts.

6. Once the performer reaches the front support position, the spotter should contact the legs to reduce any unnecessary forward motion.

1   2   3   4

1   2   3

1   2   3

Kip

1. During the forward swing, the performer should arch the back. The spotter helps by pressing forward at the lower back.

2. At the end of the forward swing, the performer flexes the hips, and draws the feet to the bar. The spotter's left hand is at the lower back to support the performer during hip flexion.

3. As the performer's legs touch the bar, the spotter pushes the hips and thighs upward. The spotter's right hand contacts the thighs.

4. The spotter's role is to provide support while the performer extends the hips to position himself in a straight-arm support position. Once the position in photo 4 is attained, the spotter maintains contact with the thighs to ensure that the performer is stable.

Reverse Grip Kip

1. The performer's hands assume the reverse grip position. That is, the palms are up instead of down (as in the regular grip). The performer arches the lower back, flexes at the hips, and raises the legs toward the bar.

2. As the legs come close to touching the bar, the hips and shoulders are again extended. The spotter can assist the performer by placing one hand under the back and the other under the thighs.

3. As the performer pulls himself up so the bar is around the hips, he grips the bar in a front support in the reverse grip position.

Mixed Grip Kip

1-2. At this point, the performer has already performed a forward swing in the arched position, as well as the initial part of the pike, with the feet moving to the bar.

3-4. As the performer begins hip flexion, the spotter contacts the lower back. Note that he is on a folded mat for better control of the performer. The performer pulls vigorously with the arms, so his legs move along the bar, up to the hips. Hip extension is an essential part of the final forward rotation of the upper body above the bar. The spotter aids the performer by supporting his legs and lower back as the performer extends the hips. Since the performer has one palm down and the other up, this skill is referred to as the "mixed grip kip."

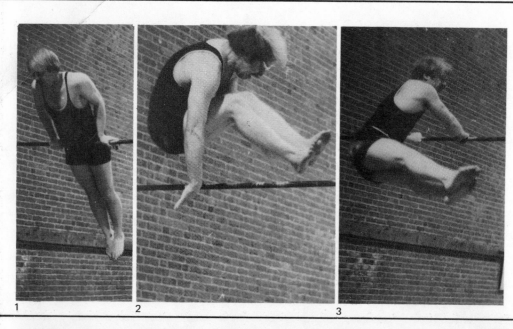

1   2   3

1   2   3

1   2   3

Flank Vault

1. The performer assumes the front support with the mixed grip. If the performer is assisted by a spotter, the bar should be lowered for the first few tries.

2. When the performer flanks with the legs to his left side, the right hand should be palm down, since it provides the final push from the bar when going over. To reach the position noted in photo 2, the performer flexes at the hips and then lifts the legs up and over the bar.

3. As the legs pass over the bar, the performer reaches back and grasps the bar with both hands. The body then straightens out. When the bar is elevated, the spotter should stand at the performer's right side to grasp the hips as they descend in step 3.

Knee Touch Dismount

1. During the upswing, the performer flexes at the hips and knees and extends the shoulders to create a tight tuck and sufficient force to raise the center of gravity further from the floor.

2. The tuck is achieved as the performer's arms are brought in to his body. Should the performer reach back to the bar after touching the knees, this skill is called the knee touch swing. The spotter should stand to the right of the performer. As the upswing is completed, the spotter reaches upward and places his right hand at the abdomen and his left hand at the lower back.

3. With the legs gradually straightened and the arms raised, the performer lands. The spotter should maintain contact with the performer on landing to help reduce the impact.

Hock Dismount

1. As the performer begins to straighten the body in step 2, the spotter places her left hand on the abdomen to help raise the upper body. Note that she has her right hand under the bar and on top of the legs. The right arm helps keep the legs flexed at the knees.

2. As the performer raises the upper body, the spotter continues to lift upward with the left hand. Once the body is reasonably high, the spotter can reduce the pressure on the legs with the right hand.

3. The spotter aids the landing with the left hand. Although this is one technique for spotting this skill, remember that another is presented for the uneven parallel bars in chapter 8. If the spotter feels that the performer may overspin, she should use the "crossed approach" on landing.

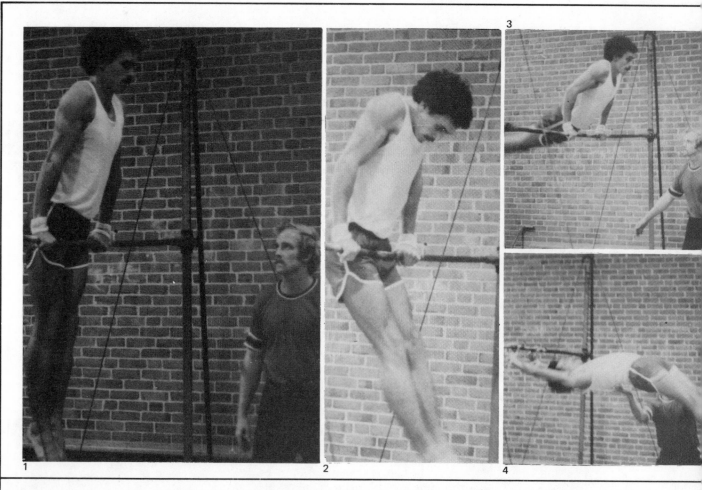

1

2

3

4

1

2

3

4

Underswing Dismount

1-2. The performer begins from the front support position, making a quick cast to increase the distance through which the center of gravity travels. The greater the distance, the more force is available to take the body up into the air.

3-4. As the legs return to and move under the bar, the shoulders quickly shift backward to allow an upward and forward continuation of the lower extremity. Note the extended position of the body at step 4. It is at this time that the spotter should contact the lower back with the right hand and the abdomen with the left.

5. If the spotter supports the lower back, the landing becomes easier. The spotter's left hand is important to keep the performer from overspinning.

Reverse Grip, Three-Quarter Giant Dismount

1. The performer flexes at the hips to produce a powerful reactive force to raise the body up and over the bar.

2. The upward motion of the legs is enhanced as the arms undergo flexion to hyperflexion at the shoulder joints. Note that the center of gravity is well above and slightly in front of the bar. The displacement of the center of gravity produces dynamic motion.

3. When the performer reaches the three-quarter position, he should flex his elbows and hips, and raise his head. At this point, the spotter should move in close to the side of the performer and assist him on landing.

4. Photo 4 shows the descent phase of the skill.

Reverse Grip Giant

1. The performer reached the position in photo 1 by flexing at the hips and casting to the inverted position.

2. As the legs and hips push away from the bar, the body continues to be extended to maximize the effects of gravity.

3. The upward motion of the second half of the skill is possible as the performer flexes at the shoulders and hips to minimize the effects of gravity. However, as the performer moves across the top of the bar, the hips should straighten.

This skill does not need to be spotted if the performer learns each aspect of the skill properly. However, if a spotter is necessary, he should stand to the side of the performer and basically under the bar. With a hesitant performer, an overhead spotting belt can also be used. The person controlling the belt must be fully aware of the proper technique for lowering the performer if he misses. Most physical education classes do not introduce the giant swings, nor do they need an overhead spotting belt.

Overgrip Giant

1. As a result of a vigorous cast to the handstand position, the performer becomes ready for the body to descend under the bar and around to the top again.

2. The performer must stretch the shoulders and body (and avoid an arch) to enhance the effect of gravity on the downward phase.

3. As the legs move into the second half of the skill, the performer must flex at the hips to decrease the radius of rotation and thus enhance angular velocity.

4. The performer can continue once again to the top (as in photo 4), or he can perform a three-quarter giant to the abdomen. In the latter case, the performer would begin with the body positioned above the bar, with the shoulders some distance in front of the hands. This particular position of the shoulder joints is indeed quite favorable for the three-quarter giant. In fact, when performing the giant swing, the shoulders should be more extended, with the arms closer to the head.

This skill, like the reverse grip giant, can be spotted without a belt. It is, however, a more difficult skill to learn than the reverse grip giant. If the performer, for example, completes only step 2 of the sequence, without finishing the full circle, then several spotters can help support him when he returns back under the bar. After using this method several times, the performer may be allowed to continue to a three-quarter giant and, perhaps, later, to a full giant swing.

12

Side Horse

The side horse event is without question a difficult apparatus to work well. The performer must be confident in his ability to master the fundamentals and the advanced skills. If he is to progress, he must be able to perform in front of others. He must set up progressive, but attainable, goals if he is to improve and maintain a high level of motivation. He must be emotionally strong and always ready to bounce back and try again. Finally, he must be motivated to try and "individualize" his performances and thus avoid limiting himself to a particular routine with a predictable style and expression. He must learn to be himself and allow his emotions and unique abilities to be expressed as he moves from one position to another on the horse.

Since spotters are not needed as frequently with this event, the primary person responsible for helping to prevent injuries is the performer. He must avoid getting on the horse until he has made sure that it is secure, stable, and surrounded with adequate mats. The pommels must be tight to reduce all extraneous movement, as well as to facilitate the side horse skills. Once the performer knows that the apparatus is safe to work on, he can still help prevent injuries by:

- wearing gymnastics pants or a warm-up suit to reduce the sudden impact of the ankles and knees during low circular motions
- making sure that the hands are reasonably well chalked to avoid a loss of grip
- approaching each exercise session with a clear and open mental frame of mind
- analyzing via basic biomechanics the specific elements and transitions required to maintain dynamic balance
- taking necessary rest intervals to allow for a rebuilding of desired energy resources

- developing a realistic daily and weekly approach to side horse work
- holding onto the horse (even if it is only with one hand) when falling
- learning how to dissipate the force of a fall via some type of a roll, if necessary
- cooperating with the spotter if his help is needed
- maintaining the desired body weight/strength ratio needed to work side horse skills

The side horse requires particularly good upper body strength. Since most student performers are generally not too strong in the shoulders and arms, the side horse can be a difficult and frustrating apparatus to work. Yet the performer can gain some tremendous benefits from working side horse skills. Besides gaining in strength and upper body development, it is emotionally very exciting to be able to stay on the pommels and perform even basic routines.

Since side horse skills are primarily dynamic and circular, they are usually performed without a spotter. This circular nature of the skills reduces the effectiveness of a spotter. Since the horse is closer to the floor than the rings, the high bar, or the parallel bars, this reduces the force factor and the possibility of injury. The illustrations will therefore depict the sequential aspect of the skills without a spotter.

The reader should also understand that the horse is traditionally divided into three parts:

1. the neck, which is always on the performer's left as he mounts the horse
2. the saddle, which is the middle of the horse between the pommels
3. the croup, which is always the part of the horse to the performer's right as he mounts the horse

These parts are identified from left to right as the performer faces the horse. This orientation does not change even when the performer turns around.

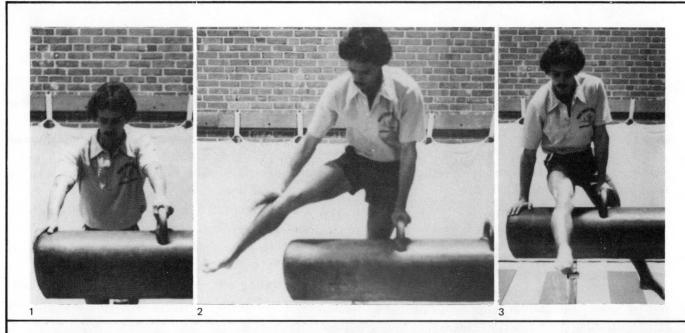

1   2   3

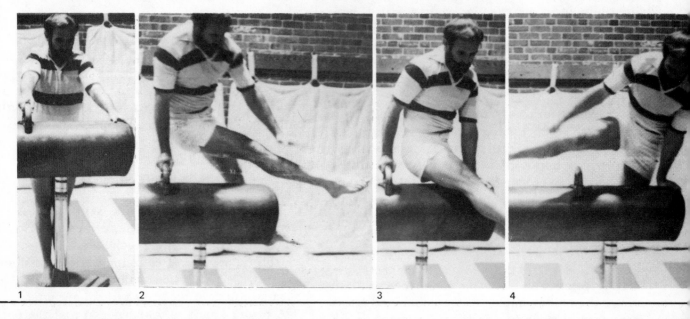

1   2   3   4

1   2   3   4

Half-Leg Circle Mount

1. Standing at the croup, the performer places his left hand on the right pommel and the right hand on the croup.

2. With a vigorous jump, the performer leans to his left, lifts the right hand, and cuts the right leg counterclockwise over the croup.

3. As the right hand contacts the croup, the right leg should be positioned between the croup and the right pommel. The left hand remains on the right pommel throughout the performance.

Undercut Full Leg Circle Mount

1. The performer should stand facing the neck, with his left hand on the neck and the right hand on the left pommel.

2. With a vigorous jump, the performer leans to the right over the left pommel, releases the left hand from the neck, and cuts the right leg under the left hand in clockwise direction.

3-4. The performer's left hand contacts the neck and again supports the body. The right leg continues a clockwise swing, as the right hand releases the left pommel (see photo 4). Note the lateral lean of the left shoulder to help keep the center of gravity over the base.

5. As the performer's right leg contacts the left leg and thus completes the circle, the right hand again contacts the left pommel to enlarge the base and finish the performance in a front support position.

Double Rear Mount to End

1-2. With the performer's right and left hands on the right and left pommels, respectively, he very vigorously jumps, while leaning over the left pommel, and cuts both legs over the croup and right pommel. Naturally, the right hand must release the right pommel to acquire the position noted in photo 2.

3-4. The counterclockwise motion of the legs continues, while the performer's center of gravity remains essentially over the left pommel. Both legs pass over the neck of the horse (step 3), and finally attain the position in photo

4. On examining the sequence, it should be clear that the left hand does not release the left pommel. Hence, the position of the left hand in step 4 is a necessary part of the skill. Also, once the right hand releases the right pommel (step 2), it remains in the air until the legs pass over the neck, when the hand contacts the neck for additional support.

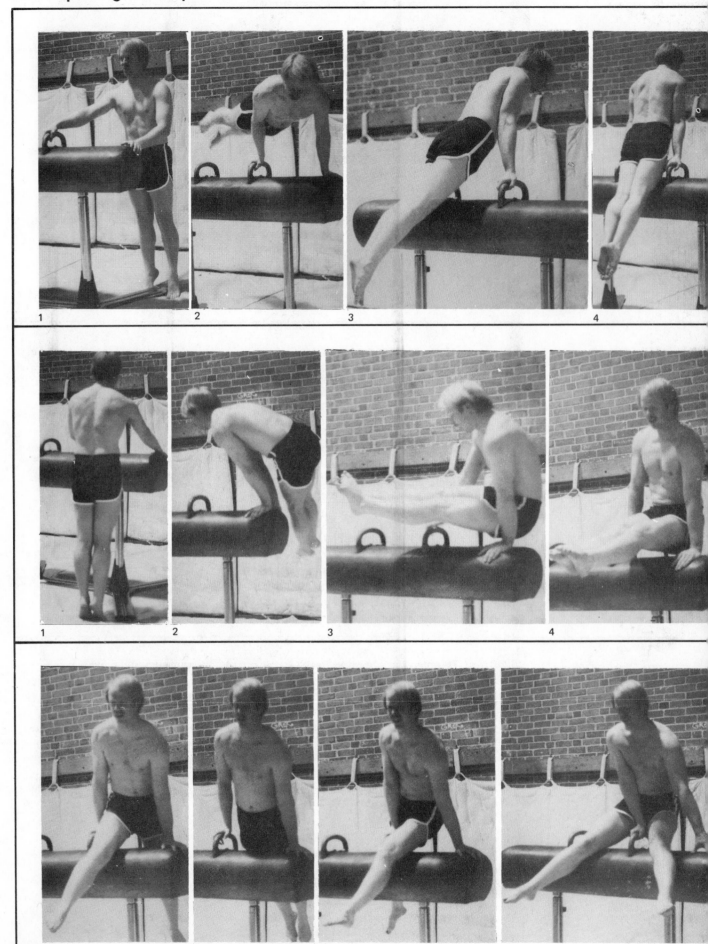

1 2 3 4

1 2 3 4

1 2 3 4

Stockli Mount

1. Standing to the side at the neck, the performer places his left hand on the neck and the right hand on the left pommel.

2-3. The performer jumps vigorously, swinging his legs counterclockwise over the croup and the right pommel. Note that the left hand adds some force to the swing via a push from the neck. The right arm must be strong enough to support the body and to maintain the swing. As the legs pass over the horse, the performer's left hand must quickly contact the right pommel.

4. The mount is finished as the performer assumes the front support. Note that the right hand of the performer does not release the pommel during the mount.

Loop Mount

1. The performer stands facing the horse, with his right hand on the croup and his left hand on the right pommel.

2-3. The moment he begins the skill, the performer quickly moves his left hand alongside the right at the croup to support the counterclockwise swing of the legs around the croup. Note that as the legs swing to the performer's right side (step 2), there is a natural lateral/forward lean of the shoulders beyond the base to keep the center of gravity as close as possible to the base. As the legs pass over the pommels, the performer's right hand reaches forward to contact the right pommel. The enlarged base allows for easier control during the final part of the skill.

4. With both hands supporting the performer, the legs are brought around directly in front of the abdomen. During the leg swing, the left hand remains at the croup.

Feint Support, Front Support, Scissor Mount

1-2. The performer's left hand is on the neck, while the right hand grasps the left pommel. The right leg is in a stride position. As the performer leans over his left hand, the right hand releases the pommel, allowing the right leg to swing clockwise to attain the front support position.

3-4. With a lean over the right hand, the performer releases the pressure from the neck. The left leg is then moved over the neck, and the left hand quickly contacts the neck again. As the hips move closer to the pommel, the performer swings his right leg over the right pommel to the scissor or straddle-feint mount position. Note that the performer's left hand may remain at the neck to maintain a reasonably large base for balance.

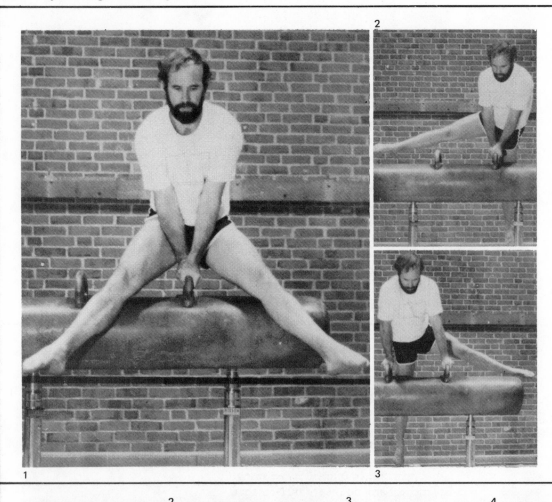

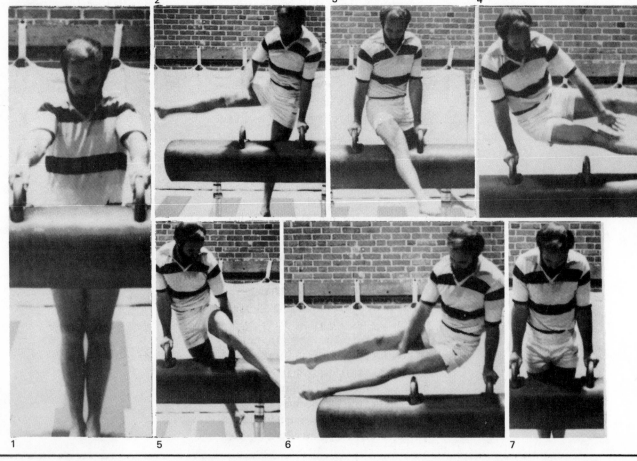

Scissor Mount with Simple Travel

1. From a scissor mount position (with both hands on the left pommel), the performer quickly swings the right leg clockwise over the right pommel.

2. Note that during the leg swing the shoulders lean to the performer's left. The moment the right leg begins to descend, the performer quickly moves his right hand from the left to the right pommel.

3. As the right hand begins to support the performer's weight, the left leg swings up and over the neck. Releasing the left hand from the left pommel allows the leg to continue its swing in a clockwise direction.

Front Scissor Mount to Front Support

1. From a frontward position at the saddle, the performer vigorously jumps to a momentary front support position.

2-3. As the performer's weight is transferred to the left arm, the right hand is raised, allowing the right leg to swing counterclockwise over the croup. Once the leg moves to the saddle, the right hand immediately contacts the right pommel again. Note the gradual upward motion of the left leg (step 3).

4-5. As the right leg moves upward to swing over the neck, the left hand is raised (step 4). While the right leg moves to a position behind the horse, the left leg moves forward to swing clockwise (step 5). During this transition it is important to maintain dynamic balance by leaning toward the right side of the right pommel. Also, the moment the left leg moves beyond the left pommel, the left hand must quickly grasp the pommel to allow for the continued shift of the shoulders from right to left.

6-7. With the clockwise swing of the left leg over the right pommel and croup, the right hand is raised to allow the legs to come together in a front support position.

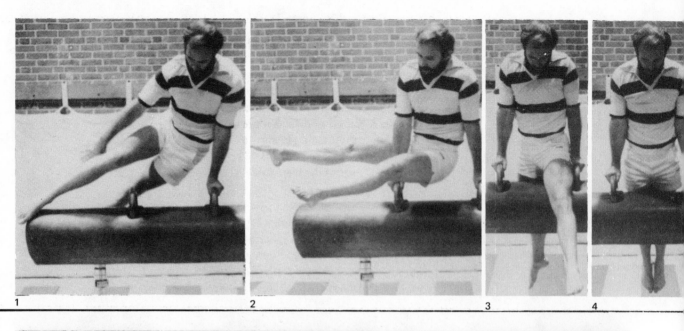

1   2   3   4

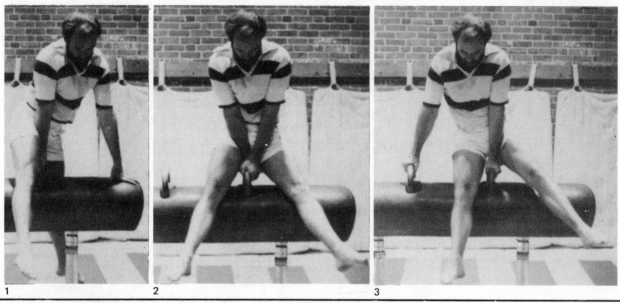

1   2   3

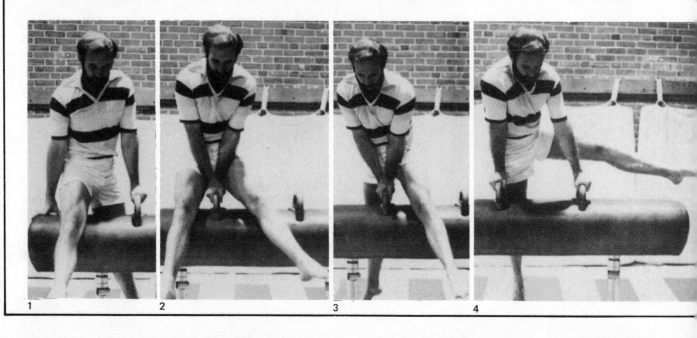

1   2   3   4

Reverse Scissor to Front Support

1-2. From a swing, supported with the left hand, the performer releases the right pommel, allowing the left leg to pass under the right leg and over the right pommel and croup. The moment the leg begins the counterclockwise motion beyond the right pommel, the performer quickly places his right hand on the pommel to insure balance.

3-4. The performer's left leg moves to a position close to the left pommel. This position of the legs, supported by both arms, is referred to as *stride* position. In step 3 the reverse scissor is completed. With the release of the left hand, the performer moves the left leg over the left pommel and neck to conclude the combination in a front support position.

Feint Support to Straddle-Feint Support

1. The feint support is a position from which the performer can effectively approach another skill or position. It is very helpful for building momentum and learning new skills. However, in this particular case, the performer is supported by both arms, with the right leg close to the left pommel. The left hand rests on the neck.

2. By raising the left hand, the performer can swing his left leg clockwise over the neck. Then the performer quickly places the left hand on the left pommel in front of the right hand.

3. From the scissors position, the performer moves his right hand to the right pommel. These are simple, but important, transitional moves that can be of assistance to beginners and intermediates in physical education classes.

Scissor Mount with Simple Travel (to Saddle)

1-2. From a stride position at the croup, the performer swings the left leg clockwise over the left pommel while grasping the right pommel with the right hand. The right hand is placed in front of the left while in the scissor mount position.

3-4. By leaning to the left, the right leg swings over the croup. As the right leg reaches a position behind the horse, the left leg moves counterclockwise over the left pommel and neck. As the left leg passes over the left pommel, the left hand is placed on the left pommel (as in photo 4).

5. After positioning the left leg alongside the right, the performer ends up in the front support position. Thus, the movement was from the croup to the saddle.

1

2

3

4

1

2

3

4

Scissor Mount with Simple Travel (to Croup)

1-2. From the scissor mount position, the performer releases the left pommel and grasps the right. He places the left hand behind the right on the right pommel. As the performer releases the left hand, his left leg moves counter-clockwise over the left pommel and neck. The right leg remains in the original position, as in step 1.

3-4. As the left leg moves to a vertical position behind the horse, the right leg swings clockwise over the croup to meet the left leg. The performer ends up in a front support position at the croup.

Scissor Mount to Full Leg Undercut

1-2. From the stride position, the performer moves his left leg forward in clockwise motion. The forward motion of the left leg is accompanied by gradual to more acute support of the body with the left arm instead of both arms (as in step 1).

3-4. As the right hand moves from the croup to the right pommel, the right leg swings vigorously clockwise over the croup, between the left leg and horse, and over the left pommel and neck to the stride position in photo 4. The undercut of the right leg is made possible with a lateral lean of the shoulders (as in photo 3).

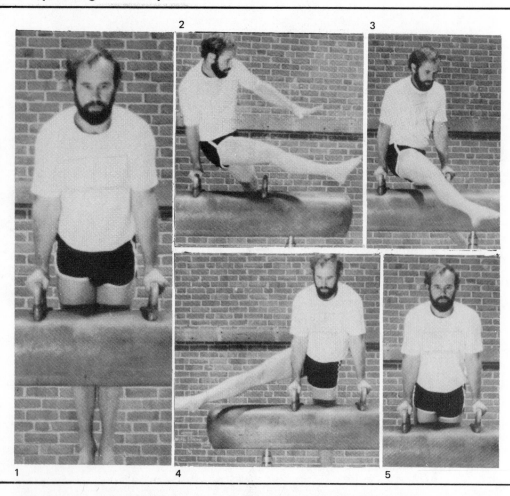

Front Support, Full Leg Circle

1. The performer acquires a front support position at the saddle.

2-3. As the left hand releases the left pommel, the performer swings the right leg clockwise over the neck. To maintain balance, the right arm is moved laterally. The left hand is positioned back on the left pommel after the right leg moves in front of the horse. Once the right leg gets close to the right pommel, the right hand is raised to allow the full circle to be completed.

4. This photo shows the placement of the right hand after the left leg swings over the pommel.

5. As the right leg moves together with the left leg, the performer again acquires the front support position.

Feint Support to Full Leg Circle, Left Leg Over

1. The performer attains the feint support position using the left pommel. While the right hand supports most of the body weight, the left hand assists by contacting the neck. This position is used to help generate the necessary force to get the legs moving together.

2-4. The performer swings the right leg clockwise over the right pommel, together with the left leg, supported mostly by the right arm. However, the leg swing continues. When the legs are brought together, this initiates the beginning of the full leg circle (with the right leg). As the legs move toward the neck, the left hand is raised to allow passage of the legs. The moment the legs pass beyond the neck, the left hand is placed back on the horse. An early contact with the left hand is necessary to allow continuation of the right leg over the left pommel (as in photo 4).

5-6. Once the right leg completes the clockwise circle, the performer moves from the stride position at the neck to a front support position.

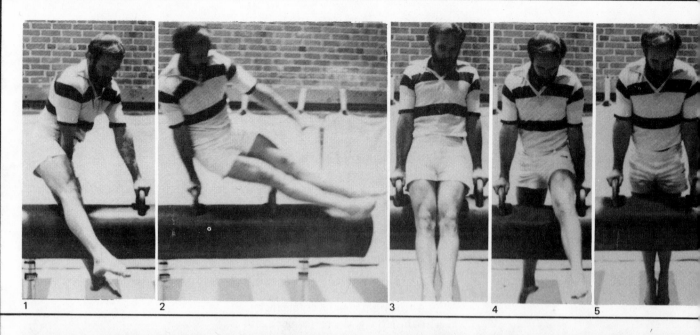

1   2   3   4   5

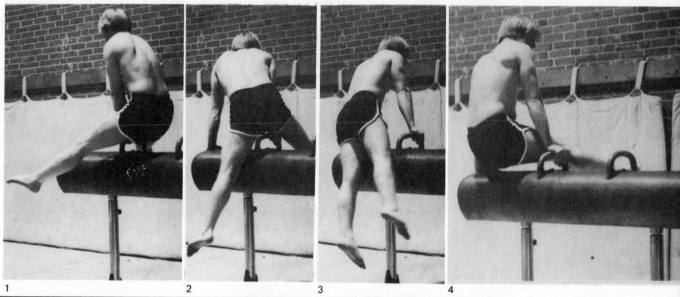

1   2   3   4

1   2   3

Feint Support to Rear Support, Right Leg Over, Left Leg Over to Front

1. The performer is positioned in a feint support position on the right pommel.

2-3. As the right leg swings clockwise over the croup to come together with the left leg, both legs move clockwise over the neck. The left hand is raised to allow passage of the legs (as illustrated in photo 2). The legs come to rest in a rear support position, but only momentarily.

4-5. The right leg continues with its clockwise motion over the croup to the stride position, noted in photo 4. By leaning on the right pommel, the performer releases the left pommel and swings the left leg counterclockwise to meet the right leg.

Feint to Three-Quarter Double Leg Circle

1. The feint is used to generate the necessary force for the performer to get started.

2-3. From the straddle position, as the performer places his left hand at the neck, the right leg is swung clockwise over the right pommel and croup. As the right leg meets the left leg, the performer leans to the right over the left pommel. He raises the left hand to allow the legs to swing over the neck and in front of the horse.

4. Both legs come to a stop in the rear support position at the neck.

Feint Support to Front Dismount

1. The performer positions himself in a feint support position over the right pommel.

2. The right leg swings over the croup, the legs are brought together, the performer releases the left pommel, leans the support arm laterally, and swings the legs clockwise over the neck.

3. The legs continue over and beyond the horse and the feet approach the floor. The right hand maintains contact with the right pommel.

Feint Support to Tromlet, Right Leg Over

1. The feint support is used to attain the force to start the double leg circle.

2. As the legs swing clockwise over the neck and left pommel, the performer raises the left hand. Note the lateral lean of the right shoulder and arm to maintain balance.

3-4. The continued clockwise motion of the legs requires releasing the right hand from the right pommel (as in photo 3). Once the legs move behind the horse, the performer must quickly position his body over the left pommel. To enhance the continuation of the skill, the right hand moves quickly to the left pommel (step 4). As the hands support the body, the legs continue the clockwise motion to pass once again over the neck.

5-6. The legs pass over the neck before the left hand contacts the neck. Yet, as soon as the legs reach a position in front of the horse, the left hand moves toward it to allow continuation of the skill.

7. As the left hand assumes a major role in supporting the body, the performer raises the left hand to allow the right leg to pass over the left pommel.

Feint Support to Triple Rear Dismount

1-2. From a feint support position on the right pommel, the performer swings the legs clockwise over the left pommel. The left hand must be raised so the legs can acquire the position in photo 2.

3-4. As the legs pass in front of the horse, the left hand quickly pushes off the left pommel, while the right hand continues to be the support arm. As the legs pass over the croup, the performer's left hand again helps support the body.

5-6. The left arm on the croup assumes major support, and the right hand is raised to allow continued clockwise motion of the legs and hips. The final part of the performance requires that the performer, on landing, keeps the left hand in contact with the horse.

7. The performer lands with hips, knees, and ankles flexed. His left hand maintains contact with the horse.

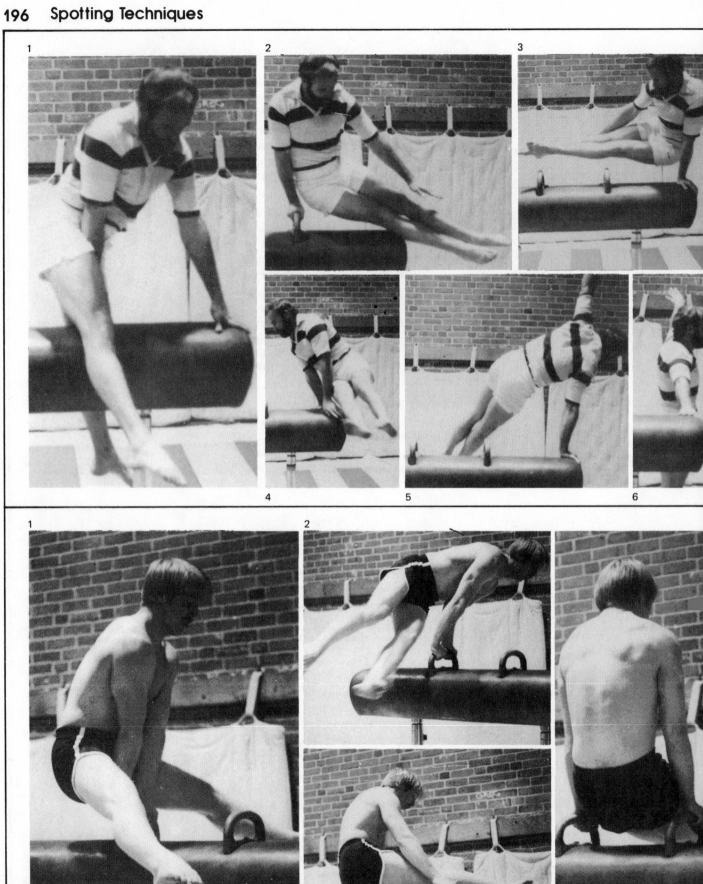

Feint Support, Double Leg Circle, Loop to Front Dismount

1-2. From a feint support position over the left pommel, the performer places the left hand at the neck to initiate the skill. The right arm supports the performer while the legs move clockwise over the neck. Note that the left hand must be raised to allow passage of the legs.

3. As the legs move in front of the horse, the left hand assumes major support, while the right hand is raised to allow the legs to move over the left pommel.

4. With the continued clockwise motion of the legs around the neck, the right hand contacts the neck and becomes the major support arm during the upward motion of the legs and hips over the horse (see photo 5).

5-6. The right hand supports the body during the final movement of the legs over and to the side of the horse. The hips should be extended during the downward phase of the performance.

On landing, the right hand should still be in contact with the neck.

Single Leg Moore

1. The performer is positioned on the left pommel, with both hands supporting the body in the straddle position.

2-4. With the performer's left hand positioned in front of the right hand, the left leg is brought vigorously over the neck to meet the right leg (step 2). Note the lateral/forward motion of the shoulders as the legs come together. Once the legs pass over the right pommel, the right hand quickly grasps the pommel, both to enlarge the base of support and to continue with the performance. The final aspect of the skill requires the performer to have a hand on each pommel.

Moore

1. From a body position that allows for continuation of the legs, the performer is supported by the right hand.

2-3. As the legs come together, the performer's left hand moves to the right pommel, both to sustain much of the weight and to control the direction of the performance. The hips must be positioned well above the croup during the counterclockwise motion shown in photos 2 and 3. Note the forward displacement of the shoulders to keep the center of gravity reasonably close to the base, the right pommel.

4. As the legs continue with the counterclockwise motion, the performer's shoulders must move back over the base to control the position of the hips and legs as they pass over the left pommel and neck. The left hand must grasp the pommel to allow for continuation of the performance.

Flank Vault

1. The spotter stands on the approach side of the horse. Note the position of the spotter's left arm.

2. As the performer contacts the horse with both hands, the spotter contacts the left forearm with her left hand. The performer flexes the hips to bring the legs horizontally over the horse, and the spotter assists with the right hand (as in photo 2).

3. As the performer descends and lands, the spotter continues to maintain contact with the left wrist until the landing is safely accomplished.

Headspring

1. The spotter stands on the mat side of the horse. Note that the spotter is well within an arm's reach of the horse.

2. The performer places both hands and her forehead on the horse and flexes the hips, keeping the legs straight. The spotter contacts the right arm with her left hand and the lower back with her right.

3. The spotter helps control the quick extension of the hips with the right hand, and upward motion of the body using the left. While the performer is airborne, the spotter should flex the knees and hips and keep the lower back straight to avoid placing too much pressure on the back area.

4. The spotter's right hand helps control the upward pressure at the lower back during the landing. To prevent the performer from overspinning, the spotter must keep a tight grip at the performer's right forearm.

Trampoline

The trampoline is an exciting part of gymnastics. Most students look forward to such skills as basic jumps, turns, seat and knee drops, and basic combinations of these. Later they can progress to intermediate skills involving twists and flips.

The trampoline, like any other apparatus in the gymnastic room, is not necessarily dangerous. But if proper teaching controls are not presented to the gymnastics class or team, it can become dangerous. At no time should a student be forced to work the trampoline. This particular apparatus should be especially chosen by the student. Moreover, the instructor should inform all students and gymnasts about the potential risks involved, as well as the need for adherence to the safety procedures. The instructor must enforce the safety rules associated with trampoline work. For example, when an instructor is not at the trampoline, spotters must always be around it when a student or an athlete is bouncing. Performers must understand that no one should attempt a new skill or begin bouncing until the instructor has given permission to do so. Finally, there must not be any playing around on the apparatus.

Trampoline work can be fun, exciting, and extremely rewarding. Since performers attain a certain amount of height on the trampoline, the force factor becomes increasingly important. The greater the force, the more the performer must maintain control to insure safety.

Hand-to-body spotting is the safest method of preventing serious injury to the neck and other areas. The safety harness is not as effective because the spotter has little control over the performer, except to keep him high above the trampoline in case of an overspin. The unfortunate result is that the performer may continue to rotate forward with little control over his body movements.

The reader will find that the first eight skills are presented without a spotter in the photographs. But do not assume that spotting and supervision are unnecessary for these skills. The spotter is especially important during the initial execution of many of the basic skills. The spotter (instructor) may spot and direct the performer from either the floor or the top of the trampoline. When spotting from the top, the spotter has more control over the performer when standing to the side or the front part of the trampoline, facing the performer. The spotter must be able to see the performer's face so he can make quick decisions and stop a performance, if necessary.

An overhead spotting device does not appear in any of the photographs, since hand spotting techniques insure adequate safety for physical education classes and gymnastics teams. Only when the skills advance to two or more twists and more than one flip should the twisting belt or the overhead spotting belt be used. Since these skills should not be introduced to physical education students, the only methods of spotting required of teachers are those illustrated in this chapter.

At present, there are no major programs or even certifying bodies that have detailed plans and procedures for teaching individuals how to become trampoline spotters. This is unfortunate, and no doubt will eventually be corrected. Unfortunately, gymnastics as a profession has placed minimal organized emphasis on spotting techniques. Physical education has also been late in realizing the need to teach undergraduate majors spotting procedures with skill progressions.

The time has come to integrate spotting techniques with their respective skills. Instructors and coaches must learn both the skills and the spotting techniques. Far too many gymnastics performers are poor instructors, and are especially weak in spotting technique. This is difficult for some parents and, perhaps, the general public to comprehend. But it is true because spotting techniques are distinctly different from gymnastics skills. This is why it is important that all gymnastics instructors demonstrate their spotting techniques to the person in charge. Without an actual demonstration of an individual's spotting skills, the person should not be allowed to spot in any gymnastics program.

1   2   3

1   2   3

Straddle Jump

This skill is often used to challenge the student who can bounce without complications. It is generally a very easy skill to execute. The performer must lean forward with the shoulders when touching the feet. If the shoulders stay back while the legs are brought up, the performer may not be able to land on her feet. Hence, the tight pike illustrated in the picture is absolutely necessary. The legs should remain straight during the descent until the feet contact the bed.

Tuck Jump

1. After the performer has practiced bouncing on the trampoline, she should be able to bounce essentially in one spot. The legs should remain straight during the upward flight, and together with the feet pointed. The arms should be somewhat horizontal to improve balance. The performer should be able to focus on the end of the trampoline while bouncing.

2. As the performer becomes airborne, the legs should be flexed at the knees and the hips.

3. The moment the performer begins to descend, the legs should be straightened while the arms are raised. On contacting the trampoline, the performer's knees should be slightly flexed to help take up the force.

Full Turn

1. As the performer leaves the trampoline during the vertical phase of the bounce, the right arm is thrown across the chest toward the left shoulder.

2. The motion of the right arm is generally necessary to enhance the full twist. The body should be slightly flexed at the hips during the twist.

3. On completing the twist, the performer ends up facing the same direction she started. The performer should not try to attain much height on this skill. Later, as the twisting mechanics are learned correctly, a greater height can be attempted.

Pike Jump

The pike jump is basically the same skill as the straddle jump, except that the performer assumes a pike position. The increased distance the performer must reach toward the feet, with the legs together, actually aids in keeping the feet under her during hip extension.

Sit Drop

The sit drop is referred to as the seat drop in many gymnastics books. From a controlled vertical bounce, the performer flexes at the hips to position the legs horizontally. The hands, as well as the legs, should contact the trampoline bed to prevent undue stress at the lower back. The hands actually push hard against the bed during the ascent phase of the sit drop. The legs must always remain straight, with the feet pointed.

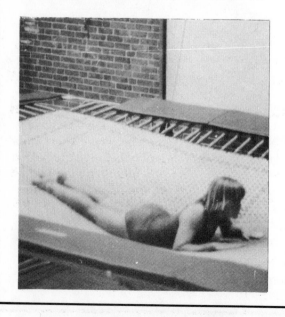

Knee Drop

The knee drop can be performed by almost every beginner. However, if a performer arches the back slightly while landing on the knees, she will experience acute pain across the back. Hence, the performer should be aware of the dangers inherent in performing this skill without the desired hip flexion. Note that the performer's hips are flexed, not only to reduce this danger, but also for reducing the force of landing. A performer who has difficulty executing this skill should position the knees about a shoulder-width apart. The feet should be pointed when landing on the knees.

Doggy Drop

The doggy drop is a modified knee drop, in which the hands are placed on the bed. Some gymnastics instructors feel this skill should be taught before the knee drop because this position automatically takes the pressure from the lower back area. An excellent method of teaching this skill is to have the performer bounce, with her hands on the knees and her feet touching the bed. On the count of three, the performer lifts her feet from the bed and leans forward, positioning the hands on the bed, with the knees touching it. The arms should remain as vertical as possible while the skill is performed.

The legs should flex at the knees, with the thighs vertical. The knees should thus assume a 90-degree angle. These place the performer in a position in which the body weight is distributed over all four points of contact.

Front Drop

In the front drop, the performer's abdomen makes contact with the trampoline bed. The contact should be such that the legs are straight (either together or slightly spread), the arms are flexed at the elbows, and the head is either held above the bed (as in the photo) or turned sideways, making contact with the bed. Girls should realize that there is no data indicating that landing on the chest will harm the breast.

An excellent and safe way to teach the front drop is from the doggy drop position, in which the performer stretches out during the ascent phase.

It can also be taught safely from the flexed knee position, in which the hands grasp the knees. On the count of three, the performer moves the feet backward to stretch out on the abdomen. The front drop can be accomplished by doing a sit drop, a doggy drop, a front drop combination, or, for more advanced performers, a sit drop, straddle the legs backward, front drop. There are various skills and combinations that are both exciting and challenging to beginning and advanced performers.

One last point, however, is that the front drop, if performed incorrectly, can cause considerable back pain. To avoid hurting the back, the teacher should encourage performers to keep their feet lower than the chest when moving into the front drop position. If the chest contacts the bed before the rest of the body, the back usually ends up hurt. This is why teachers should not encourage beginners to just throw themselves into the air and perform a front drop. While some beginners will be able to do so without complications, others will experience considerable difficulty.

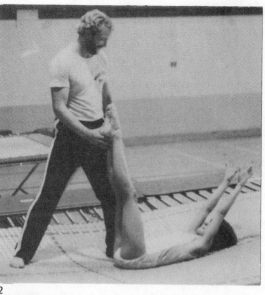

1

2

1

2

3

4

Back Flip, (A) Layout *or* (B) Pike

1-2. The performer and the spotter bounce together in preparation for the extension-tuck, and the extension-pike or the extension-layout. (The latter is shown in photo 3A). The spotter contacts the performer's lower back to control the upward motion, as well as the rotational aspect of the skill. The spotter's left hand is used, if necessary, to enhance the angular velocity of the flip.

3. Photo 3A demonstrates the layout position during the flip. Note that the legs are straight, along with a fairly straight body. The arms are generally positioned horizontally. The head is tilted backward to allow for quick visual recovery and enhancement of the backward motion. Photo 3B shows the performer in the pike position, with the hands holding the straight legs. Again, the head is extended to enhance the backward rotation and visual contact with the bed. During both types of flips (pike and layout) the performer is assisted by the spotter's right hand at the lower back area. The spotter must maintain contact throughout the flip, until the performer is safely on the trampoline in the upright position. Note that the spotter is still in contact with the bed at step 3. This is essential for proper control of the performer.

4. As the performer lands on the trampoline, both the spotter and the performer rise back into the air. For the performer, the up and down motion is continuous. But the spotter, on the other hand, must remain on the bed for one bounce and then return to the up and down motion. While in the air, the spotter maintains contact with the performer.

Barani

1. After several bounces, generally three, the performer raises the arms and pushes from the trampoline to begin the skill. The spotter places his left hand at the performer's right side or hip.

2. Once the skill is underway, the spotter's hand may leave the hips. The spotter may instead lift the performer, and then extend the right hand, from which the performer can rotate. During these maneuvers, the spotter must remain on the trampoline. Note the spotter's relatively wide stance in photo 2 to enlarge the base and thus enhance control of the performer.

3. As the performer's legs and hips begin to drop to the trampoline, the spotter may place his right hand at the performer's left side for better stabilization of the landing. For the beginning student, attempting the skill for the first time, the spotter should place a hand at the hips, just as when spotting for a cartwheel.

Front Flip, One-Half Twist

1. Photo 1 shows the spotter and the performer bouncing, just before making the last bounce before starting the skill. The spotter already has his left hand at the performer's right side.

2. The moment the performer begins the skill, the spotter flexes his knees and hips so that he stays on the trampoline. The spotter's left hand is held tight at the performer's flexed waist. The spotter's right hand is positioned so he can quickly grasp the performer's left hip or side.

3. As the performer extends from the pike position, observes the trampoline, and makes small adjustments to land, the spotter maintains control as in the picture. Both hands of the spotter support the performer and assist during the twisting action.

4. As the performer's feet contact the bed, the spotter should end up in a crossed-arm position. The spotter's left hand aids in keeping the performer from overspinning. The right hand continues to support the performer at the abdomen.

Lead-Up Progression for Full Twist Back Flip

1. The spotter contacts the performer's left side before the skill begins. After several bounces the performer extends the legs and hips and reaches backward while twisting toward the spotter.

2. The performer should be instructed to twist properly to prevent the spotter from being hit in the face with the hands. Photo 2 shows the jump one-half turn to the spotter's arms. The instructor should tell the performer to keep her legs and arms straight.

3-4. The spotter flexes at the knees and hips and allows the performer's hands to contact the bed (step 3). By placing the left hand in front of and to the right of the right hand, the performer enhances the twisting action needed to bring the feet to the trampoline. The spotter should raise the performer's body to the handstand position with his left hand (see photo 4).

5. As the performer returns her feet to the trampoline, the spotter quickly reaches for the hips, with a hand on each side to aid with the final part of the twist.

Full Twisting Back Flip

1. Before the performer leaves the trampoline, the spotter contacts the performer at the left side with his left hand.

2-3. As the performer stretches upward and turns toward the spotter, the spotter's left arm extends, first to lift the performer and then to give the performer support from which she can continue rotating. Photo 2 demonstrates the continuation of the twist toward the spotter. The spotter's left arm is held horizontally and as straight as possible to allow the performer plenty of support and room for twisting (see photo 3). Note that the spotter's legs are flexed in photo 1, while in photo 3 they are straight. The first position allows him to get under the performer, while the second helps him to lift the performer.

4. As the performer nears the vertical position, the spotter quickly moves his right hand upward to contact the performer's left hip. The spotter continues to support the performer with his left arm and shoulder.

5-6. The spotter grasps the performer's right side with his left hand. He continues to keep his right hand on the performer's left hip. These hand contacts allow the performer to land without undue pressure. On landing, the spotter releases the performer so she can straighten up. It is important to point out that this technique is potentially much better than a spotting device. The spotter has the opportunity to assist the performer physically, and to determine the specifics of the twisting action. There is more direct control of the performer when using this method, especially during the upward and beginning twist phase. This method also offers immediate control during the performer's descent to the trampoline. It does, however, require practice.

Afterword

Writing this book has been fun. I hope the illustrated spotting techniques are of value to you and your classes.

Remember, however, that these spotting techniques are skills in themselves that must be practiced over and over. You can't expect to become an excellent spotter if you don't practice and think through the mechanics of the spotting techniques. Just as it would be foolish to look at a picture of someone doing a back flip and then to try it without supervision, it can also be dangerous to attempt spotting techniques from this book without practice and supervision. You must study the photographs and apply them cautiously, if possible, with supervision.

About the Author

William T. Boone is a native of Leesville, Louisiana, where he participated in football, baseball, and track. At Northwestern State University in Natchitoches, Louisiana, he competed for four years on the gymnastics team while an undergraduate student in physical education. Following graduate school, he joined the faculty at Northeast Louisiana State University in Monroe, Louisiana, to teach physical education classes and coach the men's gymnastics team. A year later he accepted a position at the University of Florida in Gainesville to continue his gymnastics instruction. He later earned a doctoral degree in exercise physiology at Florida State University.

He is presently director of the Anatomy Laboratory at Wake Forest University in Winston-Salem, North Carolina. In addition, he is director of gymnastics at Wake Forest, where two hundred students participate in the program.

Boone has written articles on the biomechanics of gymnastics skills, the psychology of training and competition, and the specificity of energy sources in gymnastics. His articles have appeared in numerous professional journals. He is the author of the *Illustrated Handbook of Gymnastics, Tumbling, and Trampolining*, published by Parker Publishing Company, Inc., in 1976.

Recommended Reading

Gymnastics Guide edited by Hal Straus. A comprehensive, illustrated journey through men's and women's gymnastics. Physical and psychological training, safety, and profiles of champions are just a few of the areas covered. Paperback, $4.95.

Acrobatics Book by Jack Wiley. An illustrated guide to performing balancing and tumbling stunts; routines for men's pairs, women's pairs, mixed pairs, women's trios, and men's fours. Paperback, $3.95.

The Complete Diet Guide for Runners and Other Athletes by the editors of *Runner's World* magazine. How the athlete can use his diet to better advantage is the basis of this book. Areas addressed include weight control, drinks, fasting, natural vs. processed food, vegetarian diets and more. Paperback, $4.95.

Living Longer and Better by Harold Elrick, M.D., James Crakes, Ph.D., and Sam Clarke, M.S. The authors believe that traditional medical practice has mistakenly concentrated on the treatment rather than the prevention of disease. This book stresses preventing disease through proper diet and exercise. Paperback, $5.95.

Complete Weight Training Book by Bill Reynolds. Improve your athletic performance, your posture, broaden your shoulders, reduce your hips—weight training can even help you lose or gain weight. Written by one of America's most famous weight training educators, there are workout schedules for 35 different sports. Paperback, $4.95.

Runner's World Yoga Book by Jean Couch. Achieving optimum physical and psychological flexibility is possible with the help of this completely illustrated book of yoga exercise programs. Spiral binding, $7.95.

Available in fine bookstores and sport shops, or from:

World Publications, Inc.

Box 366, Mountain View, CA 94042.

Include $.45 shipping and handling for each title (maximum $2.25)